T0124238

The Characteristics and Identity of a CHRISTIAN

KAL CZOTTER

authorHOUSE®

AuthorHouse™
1663 Liberty Drive
Bloomington, IN 47403
www.authorhouse.com
Phone: 1 (800) 839-8640

Published by AuthorHouse 02/19/2016

ISBN: 978-1-5049-8065-4 (sc)
ISBN: 978-1-5049-8066-1 (e)

Library of Congress Control Number: 2016902759

Print information available on the last page.

Characteristics of a

CHRISTIAN

KAL CZOTTER

Table of Contents

The Characteristics and Identity of a Christian

The Characteristics of God

Chapter 1

The Characteristics and Identity of a Christian

The Biblical Characteristics of God

Chapter 1

God **is** Good, Loving, Forgiving, Merciful, and Peaceable. He is full of Grace and Patience. He is Compassionate, and Faithful. He is Perfectly, Righteous, Holy, and Pure. He is Gentle, Comforting, and slow to Anger and Generous. He is Kind and Truthful. He is Righteously Wrathful, Righteously Angry, Righteously Jealous, Righteously Vengeful, and He is Righteously Just. These are some of Special Revelations of the Biblical Characteristics of God, the God of Abraham, Isaac, and Jacob.

GOD IS GOOD: (Psalm 25:8) *[8] Good and upright is the Lord; therefore, he instructs sinners in the way* ***(Psalm 34:8)*** *[8] Oh, taste and see that the Lord is good! Blessed is the man who takes refuge in him!* ***(Psalm 100:5)*** *[5] For the Lord is good; his steadfast love endures forever, and his faithfulness to all generations.* ***(Psalm 106:1)*** *[1] Praise the Lord! Oh give thanks to the Lord, for he is good, for his steadfast love endures forever!*

GOD IS LOVING: (John 3:16) *[16] "For God so loved the world, that he gave his only Son, that whoever believes in him should not perish but have eternal life.* ***(Romans 8:39)*** *[39] nor height nor depth, nor anything else in all creation, will be able to separate us from the love of God in Christ Jesus our Lord.* ***(Romans 5:8)*** *[8] but God shows his love for us in that while we were still sinners, Christ died for us.* ***(1 Corinthians 2:9)***

[9] But, as it is written,
"What no eye has seen, nor ear heard,
nor the heart of man imagined,
what God has prepared for those who love him"—

(Ephesians 2:4-5) *[4] But God, being rich in mercy, because of the great love with which he loved us, [5] even when we were dead in our trespasses, made us alive together with Christ—by grace you have been saved—* ***(1 John 4:16)*** *[16] So we have come to know and to believe the love that God has for us. God is love, and whoever abides in love abides in God, and God abides in him.*

GOD IS FORGIVING: ***(Psalm 86:5)*** *[5] For you, O Lord, are good and forgiving, abounding in steadfast love to all who call upon you.* ***(Matthew 6:14-15)*** *[14] For if you forgive others their trespasses, your heavenly Father will also forgive you, [15] but if you do not forgive others their trespasses, neither will your Father forgive your trespasses.* ***(Matthew 9:5-6)*** *[5] For which is easier, to say, 'Your sins are forgiven,' or to say, 'Rise and walk'? [6] But that you may know that the Son of Man has authority on earth to forgive sins"—he then said to the paralytic— "Rise, pick up your bed and go home."* ***(1 John 1:9)*** *[9] If we confess our sins, he is faithful and just to forgive us our sins and to cleanse us from all unrighteousness.*

GOD IS MERCIFUL: (Psalm145:9) 9 *The LORD is good to all, and his mercy is over all that he has made.* ***(Nehemiah 9:27) 27*** *Therefore you gave them into the hand of their enemies, who made them suffer. And in the time of their suffering they cried out to you and you heard them from heaven, and according to your great mercies you gave them saviors who saved them from the hand of their enemies.* ***(Hebrews 8:12)*** *[12] For I will be merciful toward their iniquities, and I will remember their sins no more"* ***(Matthew 5:7)*** *[7] "Blessed are the merciful, for they shall receive mercy.* ***(Lamentations 3:22)*** *[22] The steadfast love of the LORD never ceases; his mercies never come to an end;*

GOD IS PEACEABLE: ***(2 John 1:3)*** *[3] Grace, mercy, and peace will be with us, from God the Father and from Jesus Christ the Father's Son, in truth and love.* ***(Luke 19:38)*** *[38] saying, "Blessed is the King who comes in the name of the Lord! Peace in heaven and glory in the highest!"*

(John 14:27) *[27] Peace I leave with you; my peace I give to you. Not as the world gives do I give to you. Let not your hearts be troubled, neither let them be afraid.* ***(John 16:33)*** *[33] I have said these things to you, that in me you may have peace. In the world you will have tribulation. But take heart; I have overcome the world."* ***(John 20:21)*** *[21] Jesus said to them again, "Peace be with you. As the Father has sent me, even so I am sending you."* ***(Romans 5:1) 1*** *Therefore, since we have been justified by faith, we have peace with God through our Lord Jesus Christ.*

(Romans 8:6) *[6] For to set the mind on the flesh is death, but to set the mind on the Spirit is life and peace.* ***(Romans 14:17)*** *[17] For the kingdom of God is not a matter of eating and drinking but of righteousness and peace and joy in the Holy Spirit.* ***(Romans15:33)*** *[33] May the God of peace be with you all. Amen.* ***(1 Corinthians 14:33)*** *[33] For God is not a God of confusion but of peace.*

GOD IS FULL OF GRACE: (Galatians 1:3) *[3] Grace to you and peace from God our Father and the Lord Jesus Christ,* ***(Joel 2:13)*** *[13] and rend your hearts and not your garments, "Return to the LORD your God for he is gracious and merciful· slow to anger, and abounding in steadfast love; and he relents over disaster.*

(Psalm 116:5) *[5] Gracious is the LORD, and righteous; our God is merciful.* ***(Ephesians 2:8-9)*** *[8] For by grace you have been saved through faith. And this is not your own doing; it is the gift of God, [9] not a result of works, so that no one may boast.* ***(John 1:14)*** *[14] And the Word became flesh and dwelt among us, and we have seen his glory, glory as of the only Son from the Father, full of grace and truth.* ***(John 1:16)*** *[16] For from his fullness we have all received, grace upon grace.*

(John 1:17) *[17] For the law was given through Moses; grace and truth came through Jesus Christ.* ***(Acts 15:11)*** *[11] But we believe that we will be saved through the grace of the Lord Jesus, just a they will"* ***(Acts 20:24)*** *[24] But I do not account my life of any value nor as precious to myself, if only I may finish my course and the ministry that I received from the Lord Jesus, to testify to the gospel of the grace of God.*

GOD IS PATIENT: (2 Peter 3:9) *[9] The Lord is not slow to fulfill his promise as some count slowness, but is patient toward you, not wishing that any should perish, but that all should reach repentance.* ***(James 5:8)*** *[8] also, be patient. Establish your hearts, for the coming of the Lord is hand.*

(Numbers14:19) *[19] Please pardon the iniquity of this people, according to the greatness of your steadfast love, just as you have forgiven this people, from Egypt until now."* ***(Psalm 13:5)*** *[5] But I have trusted in your steadfast love; my heart shall rejoice in your salvation.* ***(1 Timothy 1:16)*** *[16] But I received mercy for this reason, that in me, as the foremost, Jesus Christ might display his perfect patience as an example to those who were to believe in him for eternal life.*

GOD IS COMPASSIONATE: (Psalm 103:13) *[13] As a father shows compassion to his children, so the LORD shows compassion to those who fear him.* ***(Isaiah 49:13)*** *[13] Sing for joy, O heavens, and exult, O earth; break forth, O mountains, into singing! For the LORD has comforted his people and will have compassion on his afflicted.* ***(Micah 7:19)*** *[19] He will again have compassion on us; he will tread our iniquities underfoot. You will cast all our sin into the depths of the sea.*

GOD IS FAITHFUL: (1 Chronicles 16:34) *[34] Oh give thanks to the LORD, for he is good; for his steadfast love endures forever!* ***(1 John 1:9)*** *[9] If we confess our sins, he is faithful and just to forgive us our sins and to cleanse us from all unrighteousness.* ***(Hebrews 3:6)*** *[6] but Christ is faithful over God's house as a son. And we are his house if indeed we hold fast our confidence and our boasting* *in our hope* **(2 Timothy 2:12-13)** *[12] if we endure, we will also reign with him; if we deny him, he also will deny us; [13] if we are faithless, he remains faithful—for he cannot deny himself.*

(2 Thessalonians 3:3) *[3] But the Lord is faithful. He will establish you and guard you against the evil one.* **(1 Thessalonians 5:24)** *[24] He who calls you is faithful; he will surely do it.* **(1 Corinthians 10:13)** *[13] No temptation has overtaken you that is not common to man. God is faithful, and he will not let you be tempted beyond your ability, but with the temptation he will also provide the way of escape, that you may be able to endure it.*

(1 Corinthians 1:9) *[9] God is faithful, by whom you were called into the fellowship of his Son, Jesus Christ our Lord.*

GOD IS PERFECT: (Psalm 18:30) *[30] This God—his way is perfect; the word of the Lord proves true; he is a shield for all those who take refuge in him* ***(Psalm 19:7)*** *[7] The law of the Lord is perfect, reviving the soul; the testimony of the Lord is sure making wise the simple;* ***(Matthew 5:48)*** *[48] You therefore must be perfect, as your heavenly Father is perfect.*

(Deuteronomy 32:4) *[4] "The Rock, his work is perfect, for all his ways are justice. A God of faithfulness and without iniquity, just and upright is he.* **(2 Samuel 22:31)** *[31] This God—his way is perfect the word of the LORD PROVES TRUE; he is a shield for all those who take refuge in him.* ***(Psalm 50:2)*** *[2] Out of Zion, the perfection of beauty, God shines forth.* ***(Psalm 119:95-98)*** *[95] The wicked lie in wait to destroy me, but I consider your testimonies.[96] I have seen a limit to all perfection, but your commandment is exceedingly broad.[97] Oh how I love your law! It is my meditation all the day [98] Your commandment makes me wiser than my enemies, for it is ever with me.*

GOD IS RIGHTEOUS: (Psalm 7:11) *[11] God is a righteous judge, and a God who feels indignation every day.* ***(Psalm 11:7)*** *[7] For the LORD is righteous; he loves righteous deeds; the upright shall behold his face.* ***(Psalm 119: 144)*** *[144] Your testimonies are righteous* *forever; give me understanding that I may live.* ***(Isaiah 41:10)*** [10]*fear not, for I am with you; be not dismayed, for I am your God; I will strengthen you, I will help you, I will uphold you with my righteous right hand.*

GOD IS HOLY: (Leviticus 20:7) [7] *Consecrate yourselves, therefore, and be holy, for I am the LORD your God.* ***(Psalm 99:5)*** [5] *Exalt the LORD our God; worship at his footstool! Holy is he!* ***(Psalm 99:3)*** [3] *Let them praise your great and awesome name! Holy is he* ***(Psalm 111:9)*** [9] *He sent redemption to his people; he has commanded his covenant forever Holy and awesome is his name!* ***(Psalm 145:17)*** [17] *The LORD is righteous in all his ways and kind in all his works.*

GOD IS PURE: (Psalm 12:6) [6] *The words of the LORD are pure words, like silver refined in a furnace on the ground, purified seven times.* ***(Psalm 19:8)*** [8] *the precepts of the LORD are right, rejoicing the heart; the commandment of the LORD* **is pure, enlightening the eyes** ***(Matthew 5:48)*** [48] *You therefore must be perfect, as your heavenly Father is perfect.* ***(Romans 12:2)*** [2] *Do not be conformed to this world, but be transformed by the renewal of your mind, that by testing you may discern what is the will of God, what is good and acceptable and perfect.*

GOD IS GENTLE: (Matthew 11:28-29) [28] *Come to me, all who labor and are heavy laden, and I will give you rest.*[29] *Take my yoke upon you, and learn from me, for I am gentle and lowly in heart, and you will find rest for your souls. (Psalm 18:35)* [35] *You have given me the shield of your salvation, and your right hand supported me, and your gentleness made me great.*

(Jeremiah 11:19) [19] *But I was like a gentle lamb led to the slaughter. I did not know it was against me they devised schemes, saying, "Let us destroy the tree with its fruit let us cut him off from the land of the living, that his name be remembered no more."* ***(2 Corinthians 10:1) 1*** *I, Paul, myself entreat you, by the meekness and gentleness of Christ—I who am humble when face to face with you, but bold toward you when I am away! —*

GOD IS SLOW TO ANGER: (Nehemiah 9:17) *[17] They refused to obey and were not mindful of the wonders that you performed among them, but they stiffened their neck and appointed a leader to return to their slavery in Egypt. But you are a God ready to forgive, gracious and merciful, slow to anger and abounding in steadfast love, and did not forsake them.*

GOD IS THE GREAT COMFORTER: (Psalm 86:17) *[17] Show me a sign of your favor, that those who hate me may see and be put to shame because you, LORD, have helped me and comforted me.* ***(Matthew 5:4)*** *[4] "Blessed are those who mourn, for they shall be comforted* ***(2 Corinthians 1:34)*** *[3] Blessed be the God and Father of our Lord Jesus Christ, the Father of mercies and God of all comfort, [4] who comforts us in all our affliction, so that we may be able to comfort those who are in any affliction, with the comfort with which we ourselves are comforted by God.*

GOD IS GENEROUS: (Acts 14:17) 17 *Yet he has not left himself without testimony: He has shown kindness by giving you rain from heaven and crops in their seasons; he provides you with plenty of food and fills your hearts with joy."*

(Acts 15:6-9) 6 *The apostles and elders met to consider this question.* ***7*** *After much discussion, Peter got up and addressed them: "Brothers, you know that some time ago God made a choice among you that the Gentiles might hear from my lips the message of the gospel and believe.* ***8*** *God, who knows the heart, showed that he accepted them by giving the Holy Spirit to them, just as he did to us.* ***9 (Cor 8:7) 7*** *But just as you excel in everything — in faith, in speech, in knowledge, in complete earnestness and in your love for us see that you also excel in this grace of giving.* ***(Eph 1:15-18) 16*** *I have not stopped giving thanks for you, remembering you in my prayers.* ***17*** *I keep asking that the God of our Lord Jesus Christ, the glorious Father, may give you the Spirit of wisdom and revelation, so that you may know him better.* ***(Eph 5:20) 20*** *always giving thanks to God the Father for everything, in the name of our Lord Jesus Christ.*

***(Col 1:12-14)* 12** *giving thanks to the Father, who has qualified you to share in the inheritance of the saints in the kingdom of light.* **13** *For he has rescued us from the dominion of darkness and brought us into the kingdom of the Son he loves,* **14** *in whom we have redemption, the forgiveness of sins.*

GOD IS KIND: (Mark 8:38) *If anyone is ashamed of me and my words in this adulterous and sinful generation, the Son of Man will be ashamed of him when he comes in his Father's glory with the holy angels."**(Isa 54:8)** In a surge of anger I hid my face from you for a moment, but with everlasting kindness I will have compassion on you, "says the Lord your Redeemer.* ***(Jer 9:24)* 24** *but let him who boasts boast about this: that he understands and knows me, that I am the Lord, who exercises kindness, justice and righteousness on earth, for in these I delight," declares the Lord.*

***(Acts 14:17)* 17** *Yet he has not left himself without testimony: He has shown kindness by giving you rain from heaven and crops in their seasons; he provides you with plenty of food and fills your hearts with joy."*

***(Rom 2:4)* 4** *Or do you show contempt for the riches of his kindness, tolerance and patience, not realizing that God's kindness leads you toward repentance?*

***(Eph 2:4-7)* 4** *But because of his great love for us, God, who is rich in mercy,* **5** *made us alive with Christ even when we were dead in transgressions — it is by grace you have been saved.* **6** *And God raised us up with Christ and seated us with him in the heavenly realms in Christ Jesus, 7 in order that in the coming ages he might show the incomparable riches of his grace, expressed in his kindness to us in Christ Jesus.*

(1 John 3:2) [2] *Beloved, we are God's children now, and what we will be has not yet appeared; but we know that when he appears we shall be like him, because we shall see him as he is.* ***(Galatians 5:22)*** [22] *But the fruit of the Spirit is love, joy, peace, patience,* *kindness, goodness, faithfulness,* **(Jude 1:21)** [21] *keep yourselves in the love of God, waiting for the mercy of our Lord Jesus Christ that leads to eternal life.*

***GOD IS RIGHTEOUSLY WRATHFUL:* (2 Kings 22:17)** [17] *Because they have forsaken me and have made offerings to other gods, that they might provoke me to anger with all the work of their hands, therefore my wrath will be kindled against this place, and it will not be quenched.* **(Romans1:18)** [18] *For the wrath of God is revealed from heaven against all ungodliness and unrighteousness of men, who by their unrighteousness suppress the truth.*

(Romans 2:5) [5] *But because of your hard and impenitent heart you are storing up wrath for yourself on the day of wrath when God's righteous judgment will be revealed.* **(Romans 2:8)** [8] *but for those who are self-seeking and do not obey the truth, but obey unrighteousness, there will be wrath and fury.* **(Romans 9:22)** [22] *What if God, desiring to show his wrath and to make known his power, has endured with much patience vessels of wrath prepared for destruction,* **(Ecclesiastes 12:13)** [13] *The end of the matter; all has been heard. Fear God and keep his commandments, for this is the whole duty of man.*

(Ephesians 5:6) [6] *Let no one deceive you with empty words, for because of these things the wrath of God comes upon the sons of disobedience.* **(Colossians 3:6)** [6] *On account of these the wrath of God is coming.* **(1 Thessalonians 1:10)** [10] *and to wait for his Son from heaven, whom he raised from the dead, Jesus who delivers us from the wrath to come.* **(1 Thessalonians 5:9)** [9] *For God has not destined us for wrath, but to obtain salvation through our Lord Jesus Christ.*

***GOD IS RIGHTEOUSLY ANGRY:* (Judges 2:11-12)** [11] *And the people of Israel did what was evil in the sight of the LORD and served the Baals.* [12] *And they abandoned the LORD, the God of their fathers, who had brought them out of the land of Egypt. They went after other gods, from among the gods of the peoples who were around them, and bowed down to them. And they provoked the LORD to anger.*

(Psalm 30:5) [5] *For his anger is but for a moment, and his favor is for a lifetime. Weeping may tarry for the night but joy comes with the morning.* ***(Psalm27:9) 9*** *Hide not your face from me. Turn not your servant away in anger, O you who have been my help. Cast me not off; forsake me not, O God of my salvation!*

GOD IS RIGHTEOUSLY JEALOUS: (Deuteronomy 6:15-16) [15] *for the Lord your God in your midst is a jealous God—lest the anger of the Lord your God be kindled against you, and he destroy you from off the face of the earth.* [16] *"You shall not put the LORD your God to the test, as you tested him at Massah. (Exodus 34:14)* [14] *(for you shall worship no other god, for the Lord, whose name is Jealous, is a jealous God),*

GOD IS RIGHTEOUSLY VENGEFUL: (Romans 12:19) [19] *Beloved, never avenge yourselves, but leave it to the wrath of God, for it is written, "Vengeance is mine, I will repay, says the Lord."*

(2 Thessalonians 1:6-8) [6] *since indeed God considers it just to repay with affliction those who afflict you,* [7] *and to grant relief to you who are afflicted as well as to us, when the Lord Jesus is revealed from heaven with his mighty angels* [8] *in flaming fire, inflicting vengeance on those who do not know God and on those who do not obey the gospel of our Lord Jesus.* ***(Luke 21:20-22)*** [20] *"But when you see Jerusalem surrounded by armies, then know that its desolation has come near.* [21] *Then let those who are in Judea flee to the mountains, and let those who are inside the city depart, and let not those who are out in the country enter it,* [22] *for these are days of vengeance, to fulfill all that is written.*

GOD IS RIGHTEOUSLY JUST: (Matthew 5:45) [45] *so that you may be sons of your Father who is in heaven. For he makes his sun rise on the evil and on the good, and sends rain on the just and on the unjust.* ***(Matthew 12:18)*** [18] *"Behold, my servant whom I have chosen, my beloved with whom my soul is well pleased. I will put my Spirit upon him, and he will proclaim justice to the Gentiles.* ***(Deuteronomy 32:4)*** [4] *"The Rock, his work is perfect, for all his ways are justice A God of faithfulness and without iniquity, just* *and upright is he.* ***(Isaiah 30:18)***[18] *Therefore the* L*ORD waits to be gracious to you, and therefore he exalts himself to show mercy to you. For the* L*ORD* ***is a God of justice;*** *blessed are all those who wait for him.* ***(Luke 15:10)*** [10] *Just so, I tell you, there is joy before the angels of God over one sinner who repents."* ***(Romans 8:33)*** [33] *Who shall bring any charge against God's elect? It is God who justifies.*

GOD IS TRUTHFUL: (John 3:31-36) 31 *"The one who comes from above is above all; the one who is from the earth belongs to the earth, and speaks as one from the earth. The one who comes from heaven is above all.* ***32*** *He testifies to what he has seen and heard, but no one accepts his testimony.* ***33*** *The man who has accepted it has certified that God is truthful.* ***34*** *For the one whom God has sent speaks the words of God, for God gives the Spirit without limit.* ***35*** *The Father loves the Son and has placed everything in his hands.* ***36*** *Whoever believes in the Son has eternal life, but whoever rejects the Son will not see life, for God's wrath remains on him."*

(Ps 31:5) 5 *Into your hands I commit my spirit; redeem me, O Lord, the God of truth.*

(John 14:6-7) 6 *Jesus answered, "I am the way and the truth and the life. No one comes to the Father except through me.* ***7*** *If you really knew me, you would know my Father as well. From now on, you do know him and have seen him.* ***(John 15:26-27) 26*** *"When the Counselor comes, whom I will send to you from the Father, the Spirit of truth who goes out from the Father, he will testify about me.* ***27*** *And you also must testify, for you have been with me from the beginning.* ***(John 16:13) 13*** *But when he, the Spirit of truth, comes, he will guide you into all truth. He will not speak on his own; he will speak only what he hears, and he will tell you what's to come.*

The Characteristics and Identity of a Christian

Biblical Characteristics of Man

Chapter 2

The Characteristics and Identity of a Christian

Biblical Characteristics of Man

Chapter 2

The characteristics of man are that he has sinful appetites, fleshly lusts, and an evil heart that is carnal. Man is a lover of sin and because of this, he is filthy and defiled, his mind is sinful, his thoughts are sinful, and his imagination is sinful. Therefore, man has evil passions. His flesh is lustful as are his eyes lustful as well. Therefore, his nature is carnal; and sinful, and without self-control, suppressing the truth. He feeds his appetites and even further rejects putting to death the old self and following Jesus. Without doing this, we will remain the old self and sinful by nature. We must put on the new self and clothe ourselves in Christ. Amen

Self-Denial

(Matt 16:24-26)[24] ***Then Jesus said to his disciples, "If anyone would come after me, he must deny himself and take up his cross and follow me.*** [25] ***For whoever wants to save his life will lose it, but whoever loses his life for me will find it.*** (Luke 14:27) ***And anyone who does not carry his cross and follow me cannot be my disciple.*** (Luke 14:25-26) [26] ***"If anyone comes to me and does not hate his father and mother, his wife and children, his brothers and sisters — yes, even his own life — he cannot be my disciple.*** [2](Luke 14:28) [28] ***"Suppose one of you wants to build a tower. Will he not first sit down and estimate the cost to see if he has***

enough money to complete it? (Gal5:24) ***24 Those who belong to Christ Jesus have crucified the sinful nature with its passions and desires.***

Follow Christ

(Phil 3:8-9) ***8 What is more, I consider everything a loss compared to the surpassing greatness of knowing Christ Jesus my Lord, for whose sake I have lost all things. I consider them rubbish, that I may gain Christ.*** (Luke 18:28)***28 Peter said to him, "We have left all we had to follow you!"*** (Luke 14:33) ***33 In the same way, any of you who does not give up everything he has cannot be my disciple.*** (Luke 5:27-28) ***27 After this, Jesus went out and saw a tax collector by the name of Levi sitting at his tax booth. "Follow me," Jesus said to him, 28 and Levi got up, left everything and followed him.***

Suppressing Our Appetites

(Luke 12:22-22)***22 Then Jesus said to his disciples: "Therefore I tell you, do not worry about your life, what you will eat; or about your body, what you will wear. 23 Life is more than food, and the body more than clothes. (Matt 6:33)33 But seek first his kingdom and his righteousness, and all these things will be given to you as well.*** (Luke 21:34-35) ***34 "Be careful, or your hearts will be weighed down with dissipation, drunkenness and the anxieties of life, and that day will close on you unexpectedly like a trap.*** (1 Cor 9:26-27)***27 No, I beat my body and make it my slave so that after I have preached to others, I myself will not be disqualified for the prize.***

Old Self

(Rom 6:5-7)***6 For we know that our old self was crucified with him so that the body of sin might be done away with, that we should no longer be slaves to sin— 7 because anyone***

who has died has been freed from sin. (Eph 4:21-24) ***22 You were taught, with regard to your former way of life, to put off your old self, which is being corrupted by its deceitful desires; 23 to be made new in the attitude of your minds; 24 and to put on the new self, created to be like God in true righteousness and holiness.*** (Col 3:9) ***Do not lie to each other, since you have taken off your old self with its practices*** (1 Peter 4:3) ***3 For you have spent enough time in the past doing what pagans choose to do — living in debauchery, lust, drunkenness, orgies, carousing and detestable idolatry.***

Subdue Fleshly Lust

(Matt 5:27-30) ***27 "You have heard that it was said, 'Do not commit adultery.' 28 But I tell you that anyone who looks at a woman lustfully has already committed adultery with her in his heart. 29 If your right eye causes you to sin, gouge it out and throw it away. It is better for you to lose one part of your body than for your whole body to be thrown into hell.*** (Rom 13:14) ***14 Rather, clothe yourselves with the Lord Jesus Christ, and do not think about how to gratify the desires of the sinful nature.***

(Gal 5:24-26) ***24 Those who belong to Christ Jesus have crucified the sinful nature with its passions and desires. 25 Since we live by the Spirit, let us keep in step with the Spirit.***

(Col 3:5-11) ***death, therefore, whatever belongs to your earthly nature: sexual immorality, impurity, lust, evil desires and greed, which is idolatry. 6 Because of these, the wrath of God is coming. 7 You used to walk in these ways, in the life you once lived. 8 But now you must rid yourselves of all such things as these: anger, rage, malice, slander, and filthy language from your lips. 9 Do not lie to each other, since you have taken off your old self with its practices 10 and have put on the new self, which is being renewed in knowledge in the image of its Creator.***

(1 Peter 2:11-12) ***11 Dear friends, I urge you, as aliens and strangers in the world, to abstain from sinful desires, which war against your soul. 12 Live such good lives among the pagans that, though they accuse you of doing wrong, they may see your good deeds and glorify God on the day he visits us.*** (1 Peter 4:1-2) ***4 Therefore, since Christ suffered in his body, arm yourselves also with the same attitude, because he who has suffered in his body is done with sin. 2 As a result, he does not live the rest of his earthly life for evil human desires, but rather for the will of God.***

The Evil Heart of Man

(Jer 17:9-10) ***9 The heart is deceitful above all things and beyond cure. Who can understand it? 10 "I the Lord search the heart and examine the mind, to reward a man according to his conduct, according to what his deeds deserve."***

(Matt 23:25-26) ***25 "Woe to you, teachers of the law and Pharisees, you hypocrites! You clean the outside of the cup and dish, but inside they are full of greed and self-indulgence. 26 Blind Pharisee! First clean the inside of the cup and dish, and then the outside also will be clean.*** (Gen 6:5-6) ***5 The Lord saw how great man's wickedness on the earth had become, and that every inclination of the thoughts of his heart was only evil all the time. 6 The Lord was grieved that he had made man on the earth, and his heart was filled with pain.***

(Heb 3:12-13) ***12 See to it, brothers, that none of you has a sinful, unbelieving heart that turns away from the living God.***

Carnal Man

(John 6:26-27) ***26 Jesus answered, "I tell you the truth, you are looking for me, not because you saw miraculous signs but because you ate the loaves and had your fill. 27 Do not work for food that spoils, but for food that endures to***

eternal life, which the Son of Man will give you. On him God the Father has placed his seal of approval

(Rom 7:22-25) ***22 For in my inner being I delight in God's law; 23 but I see another law at work in the members of my body, waging war against the law of my mind and making me a prisoner of the law of sin at work within my members. 24 What a wretched man I am! Who will rescue me from this body of death?***

(Gal 5:13-14) ***13 You, my brothers, were called to be free. But do not use your freedom to indulge the sinful nature; rather, serve one another in love.*** (1 John 2:4-6) ***5 But if anyone obeys his word, God's love is truly made complete in him. This is how we know we are in him: 6 Whoever claims to live in him must walk as Jesus did.***

Man's Love of sin

(Job 15:16) ***16 how much less man, who is vile and corrupt, who drinks up evil like water!*** (Ps 52:3-4) ***3 You love evil rather than good, falsehood rather than speaking the truth. 4 You love every harmful word, O you deceitful tongue!*** (Prov 2:14-15) ***14 who delight in doing wrong and rejoice in the perverseness of evil, 15 whose paths are crooked and who are devious in their ways.***

(2 Thess 2:11-12) ***11 For this reason God sends them a powerful delusion so that they will believe the lie 12 and so that all will be condemned who have not believed the truth but have delighted in wickedness.***

Filthy man

(Ps 53:3)
3 Everyone has turned away,
they have together become corrupt;
there is no one who does good,
not even one.

(Matt 23:27-28) [27] *"Woe to you, teachers of the law and Pharisees, you hypocrites! You are like whitewashed tombs, which look beautiful on the outside but on the inside are full of dead men's bones and everything unclean.* [28] *In the same way, on the outside you appear to people as righteous but on the inside you are full of hypocrisy and wickedness.*

(Rom 6:19-20) [19] *I put this in human terms because you are weak in your natural selves. Just as you used to offer the parts of your body in slavery to impurity and to ever-increasing wickedness, so now offer them in slavery to righteousness leading to holiness.*

(Eph 5:3-7) [3] *But among you there must not be even a hint of sexual immorality, or of any kind of impurity, or of greed, because these are improper for God's holy people.* [4] *Nor should there be obscenity, foolish talk or coarse joking, which are out of place, but rather thanksgiving.* [5] *For of this you can be sure: No immoral, impure or greedy person — such a man is an idolater — has any inheritance in the kingdom of Christ and of God.* [6] *Let no one deceive you with empty words, for because of such things God's wrath comes on those who are disobedient.* (James 1:21)[21] *Therefore, get rid of all moral filth and the evil that is so prevalent and humbly accept the word planted in you, which can save you.* (2 Peter 2:10) [10] *This is especially true of those who follow the corrupt desire of the sinful nature and despise authority.*

Defiled man

(Isa 59:3-4) [3] *For your hands are stained with blood, your fingers with guilt. Your lips have spoken lies, and your tongue mutters wicked things.* [4] *No one calls for justice; no one pleads his case with integrity. They rely on empty arguments and speak lies; they conceive trouble and give birth to evil.*

(Mark 7:20-23) [20] ***He went on: "What comes out of a man is what makes him 'unclean.'*** [21] ***For from within, out of men's hearts, come evil thoughts, sexual immorality, theft, murder, adultery,*** [22] ***greed, malice, deceit, lewdness, envy, slander, arrogance and folly.*** [23] ***All these evils come from inside and make a man 'unclean.'"***

(Heb 12:14-17) [14] ***Make every effort to live in peace with all men and to be holy; without holiness no one will see the Lord.*** [15] ***See to it that no one misses the grace of God and that no bitter root grows up to cause trouble and defile many.*** [16] ***See that no one is sexually immoral, or is godless like Esau, who for a single meal sold his inheritance rights as the oldest son.*** [17] ***Afterward, as you know, when he wanted to inherit this blessing, he was rejected. He could bring about no change of mind, though he sought the blessing with tears***

Man's Sinful Mind

(Rom 1:28-29) ***28 Furthermore, since they did not think it worthwhile to retain the knowledge of God, he gave them over to a depraved mind, to do what ought not to be done. 29 They have become filled with every kind of wickedness, evil, greed and depravity.*** (Rom 8:7-8) ***7 the sinful mind is hostile to God. It does not submit to God's law, nor can it do so. 8 Those controlled by the sinful nature cannot please God.***

(Eph 4:17-21) ***17 So I tell you this, and insist on it in the Lord, that you must no longer live as the Gentiles do, in the futility of their thinking. 18 They are darkened in their understanding and separated from the life of God because of the ignorance that is in them due to the hardening of their hearts. 19 Having lost all sensitivity, they have given themselves over to sensuality so as to indulge in every kind of impurity, with a continual lust for more. 20 You, however, did not come to know Christ that way.***

(Titus 1:15-16) ***15 To the pure, all things are pure, but to those who are corrupted and do not believe, nothing is pure. In fact, both their minds and consciences are corrupted. 16 They claim to know God, but by their actions they deny him. They are detestable, disobedient and unfit for doing anything good.***

Man's Evil Thoughts

(Ps 64:6)***6 They plot injustice and say, "We have devised a perfect plan! Surely the mind and heart of man are cunning.*** (Ps 94:11) ***11 The Lord knows the thoughts of man; he knows that they are futile.*** (Prov 15:26) 26 The ***Lord detests the thoughts of the wicked, but those of the pure are pleasing to him.***

(Matt 15:19) ***19 For out of the heart come evil thoughts, murder, adultery, sexual immorality, theft, false testimony, slander.***

Man's Evil Imagination

(Gen 6:5)***5 The Lord saw how great man's wickedness on the earth had become, and that every inclination of the thoughts of his heart was only evil all the time.***

(Ps 38:12)***12 Those who seek my life set their traps, those who would harm me talk of my ruin; all day long they plot deception.*** (Prov 6:16-20)***6 There are six things the Lord hates, seven that are detestable to him: 17 haughty eye a lying tongue, hands that shed innocent blood, 18 a heart that devises wicked schemes, feet that are quick to rush into evil, 19 a false witness who pours out lies and a man who stirs up dissension among brothers.***

(Rom 1:21-25) ***21 For although they knew God, they neither glorified him as God nor gave thanks to him, but their***

thinking became futile and their foolish hearts were darkened. 22 Although they claimed to be wise, they became fools 23 and exchanged the glory of the immortal God for images made to look like mortal man and birds and animals and reptiles. 24 Therefore God gave them over in the sinful desires of their hearts to sexual impurity for the degrading of their bodies with one another. 25 They exchanged the truth of God for a lie, and worship and served created things rather than the Creator — who is forever praised. Amen.

Man's Evil Passions

(Rom 1:26-27) ***26 Because of this, God gave them over to shameful lusts. Even their women exchanged natural relations for unnatural ones. 27 In the same way the men also abandoned natural relations with women and were inflamed with lust for one another. Men committed indecent acts with other men, and received in themselves the due penalty for their perversion.*** (Rom 7:4-5) ***4 So, my brothers, you also died to the law through the body of Christ, that you might belong to another, to him who was raised from the dead, in order that we might bear fruit to God. 5 For when we were controlled by the sinful nature, the sinful passions aroused by the law were at work in our bodies, so that we bore fruit for death.*** (Gal 5:24) ***24 Those who belong to Christ Jesus have crucified the sinful nature with its passions and desires.*** (1 Thess 4:2-5) ***2 For you know what instructions we gave you by the authority of the Lord Jesus. 3 It is God's will that you should be sanctified: that you should avoid sexual immorality; 4 that each of you should learn to control his own body in a way that is holy and honorable, 5 not in passionate lust like the heathen, who do not know God;***

Man's Sinful Lust

(Prov 6:23-25) ***23 For these commands are a lamp, this teaching is a light, and the corrections of discipline are the way to life, 24 keeping you from the immoral woman, from the smooth tongue of the wayward wife. 25 Do not lust in your heart after her beauty or let her captivate you with her eyes,*** (Matt 5:27-29) ***28 But I tell you that anyone who looks at a woman lustfully has already committed adultery with her in his heart.*** (Gal 5:16-17) ***16 So I say, live by the Spirit, and you will not gratify the desires of the sinful nature.*** (Col 3:5) ***5 Put to death, therefore, whatever belongs to your earthly nature: sexual immorality, impurity, lust, evil desires and greed, which is idolatry.*** (1 Thess 4:4-5) ***that each of you should learn to control his own body in a way that is holy and honorable, 5 not in passionate lust like the heathen, who do not know God;***

(2 Tim 2:20-23)***21 If a man cleanses himself from the latter, he will be an instrument for noble purposes, made holy, useful to the Master and prepared to do any good work.22 Flee the evil desires of youth, and pursue righteousness, faith, love and peace, along with those who call on the Lord out of a pure heart.*** 1 Peter 2:11) ***11 Dear friends, I urge you, as aliens and strangers in the world, to abstain from sinful desires, which war against your soul.***

Man's Lustful Eyes

(2 Sam 11:2-5) ***2 It happened, late one afternoon, when David arose from his couch and was walking on the roof of the king's house, that he saw from the roof a woman bathing; and the woman was very beautiful. 3 And David sent and inquired about the woman. And one said, "Is not this Bathsheba, the daughter of Eliam, the wife of Uriah the Hittite?" 4 So David sent messengers and took her, and she came to him, and he lay with her. (N Now she had been***

purifying herself from her uncleanness.) Then she returned to her house. 5 And the woman conceived, and she sent and told David, "I am pregnant."

(Job 31:1) ***1 "I made a covenant with my eyes not to look lustfully at a girl.*** (Matt 5:28-29) ***28 But I tell you that anyone who looks at a woman lustfully has already committed adultery with her in his heart.*** (1 John 2:15-17) ***16 For everything in the world — the cravings of sinful man, the lust of his eyes and the boasting of what he has and does — comes not from the Father but from the world. 17 The world and its desires pass away, but the man who does the will of God lives forever.***

Man's Carnal Nature

(Rom 7:17-20) ***18 I know that nothing good lives in me, that is, in my sinful nature. For I have the desire to do what is good, but I cannot carry it out. 19 For what I do is not the good I want to do; no, the evil I do not want to do — this I keep on doing. 20 Now if I do what I do not want to do, it is no longer I who do it, but it is sin living in me that does it.***

(Gal 5:16-17) ***17 For the sinful nature desires what is contrary to the Spirit, and the Spirit what is contrary to the sinful nature. They are in conflict with each other, so that you do not do what you want*** (Gal 6:7-8) ***8 The one who sows to please his sinful nature, from that nature will reap destruction; the one who sows to please the Spirit, from the Spirit will reap eternal life.*** (Rom 8:12-15) ***13 For if you live according to the sinful nature, you will die; but if by the Spirit you put to death the misdeeds of the body, you will live, 14 because those who are led by the Spirit of God are sons of God. 15 For you did not receive a spirit that makes you a slave again to fear, but you received the Spirit of sonship. And by him we cry, "Abba, Father."***

The Characteristics and Identity of a Christian

Biblical Characteristics of the Christian

Chapter 3

The Characteristics and Identity of a Christian

Biblical Characteristics of the Christian

Chapter 3

(*Rom 8:28-29*)***28 And we know that in all things <u>God works</u> for the <u>good</u> of those who love him, who have been <u>called</u> according to his purpose. 29 For those God <u>foreknew</u> he also <u>predestined</u> to be <u>conformed</u> to the likeness of his Son, that he might be the <u>firstborn</u> among many brothers.***

- This is the Truth of God's Word: ***For those God foreknew he also predestined to be conformed to the likeness of his Son***

I speak from my heart to tell you, the reader, the Truth of God's Word in the following chapters. In this chapter we will look at the importance of the Father's desire, passion, and love and how we will adopt His characteristics in seeking to be more like Him.

We read in Holy Scripture:

(Heb 1:3-5) This text speaks about Jesus ***3 <u>The Son is the radiance of God's glory</u> and the exact representation of his being, sustaining all things by his powerful word. After he had provided purification for sins, he sat down at the right hand of the Majesty in heaven.***

<u>The Son is the radiance of God's glory</u> the first thing we need to do, is gain an understanding of the Father's desires, passions, and love that we can adopt them to be more like Him today.

Desires

- The Father desires us to conform to Jesus' Way, by adopting His Character.
- The Father desires us to know Him more intimately as His Children.
- The Father desires us to know His Fatherhood more intimately
- The Father desires u to know His Love more intimately.

Our desires have changed from being self-seeking, to becoming co-labourers with the Holy Spirit being zealous to fulfill the Father's desires.

- We do this by desiring His Character and valuing His Character that our values match His Values, that our character matches His Character, and that our moral and ethical law matches His and Moral and Ethical law. This is His desire that we forsake our way and adopt His Way.

Passion

Our Father's passion is for the lost, the deaf and the blind. His passion is for the poor, the fatherless, and the widowed. His passion is for the lame, the sick, the crippled, the elderly, and the single parents, as well the repentant. His passion is for the one in jail, the hungry, and the thirsty, the homeless, the weak, the mourner, the orphan, the lonely, the foreigner, the sojourner, the spiritually dead, the contrite in heart, the humble, the meek and the peacemakers of the earth, the wise, the faithful, the loyal, the just, the righteous, the holy, and the Godly.

Our Father's passion is to reconcile everything to Him that none should perish.

Our passion should be to reconcile everything to Him that none should perish.

- He is fully invested in His saving enterprise this is His passion, He has invested everything: His Son, His Spirit, His Word and His labour and yes even His labourer's.
- His Saving Enterprise is His Passion!
- We should invest ourselves in His passion with our:
- Time
- Talent
- Treasures.

His passion will be our passion, with the motive of love, drawing people to Jesus to receive redemption and the forgiveness of sins.

Love

We know that the Father loves us, because He loved us first, and when we did not have it in ourselves to love Him, He loved us and showed Himself, to us.

- The Father's love is for the Son.
- The Father's love is for His adopted children.
- The Father loves us cheerfully and with joy when we repent of our wrongs.

He showed Himself, to us.

- We can give a clear testimony to His love.
- We know the Father has given an example how to love one another.
- This is a start friends. **God's Word!**

The Father's Love, passion, and desires are rooted in the Father's purpose, plan, and Will

We will ponder this.

Jesus is the ***firstborn among many brothers*** and we have hope in the cross, the sinless life of Jesus Christ, that He alone, imputed to us who believe as a gift by God`s Grace. In this chapter we see that God's Truth, His Love, and His Grace have changed our hearts. He is changing our desires, our passions and our love.

Every Born Again Christian know that God's love has been revealed to us and we are changing because of His love.

- We are changed dramatically.
- We are softening our hearts to God.
- We are a work in progress.
- We are repenting our sins.
- We are putting on Jesus' Character more and more.
- We are adopting our Father's purpose, plan, and Will for our lives in order to bring Him Glory.

May He work in us what is pleasing to him!!!

***(John 10:27-30)* says: *My sheep listen to my voice; I know them, and they follow me. 28 I give them eternal life, and they shall never perish; no one can snatch them out of my hand. 29 My Father, who has given them to me, is greater than all; no one can snatch them out of my Father's hand. 30 I and the Father are one.*"**

Just as Jesus is one with the Father, we will be one with the Father; we will be one within His purpose, plan, and Will.

Thus, our Father has set forth His purpose, plan, and Will

1. Our Father has set forward His purpose and only the willing heart will submit to His purpose: which is His saving enterprise.
2. Our Father has set forward His plan and only the willing heart will submit to His plan: which is the Trinity's Redemptive Plan: the plan to seek and save the lost and draw all humankind to God their Father, and He will give us to His Son as a love gift to receive redemption and the forgiveness of sin. Then the Son will return reconciling us back to the Father sanctified, fashioned,

and beautified, enabled by the Holy Spirt that we may glorify Him and enjoy Him forever.

3. Finally, our Father has set forth His will and only the willing heart will submit to His will: which is our sanctification, our holiness, and our consecration.

We have been saved from the final judgment, and have been justified

- We have been reconciled to the Father then we are made by Him, to be more like Him.
- He does this by changing our hearts desires, passions, and love so they come into alignment with His purposes, plan, and Will.
- We accomplished this by adopting His Character and His likeness.

We should desire God's Character

- We should desire to be part of His Saving Enterprise.
- We should have passion in conforming to the Likeness of His Character.
- We should love winning souls to Jesus.

This is the Father's workmanship in us

(Ezek 36:25-28) 25 I will sprinkle clean water on you, and you will be clean; I will cleanse you from all your impurities and from all your idols. 26 I will give you a new heart and put a new spirit in you; I will remove from you your heart of stone and give you a heart of flesh. 27 And I will put my Spirit in you and move you to follow my decrees and be careful to keep my laws.

Christians, we have been transferred into the Kingdom of Light out of the domain of darkness. "It is finish!" now, live this Truth of God`s Word out!

Be quick to forgive one another,

be quick to love one another,
be quick to pray for one another
Kal Czotter

Just like Jesus who forgave us, loved us, and prayed for us. We will do the same until the Lord returns by adopting Jesus' Character. Remember faith believes God Word and the immutable, inerrant, infallible, and impeccable; Truth of His Word! Amen

The Father's Will is to save us, and reconcile us; and conform us, that we bear the Image and Likeness of Him and His Character in this chapter I am going to reveal the Father's Character and that we can adopt His Character today***; this is impossible, but with God all things are possible***.

(Matt 3:17) And a voice from heaven said, "This is my Son, whom I love; with him I am well pleased."

As we associate our lives with God, we are made by Him to be more like Him.

- We glorify the Father by mirroring His Character to the fallen world around us, as His representatives and when His Son returns The Father will glorify the workmanship of His hands.
- We are the workmanship of His Hand alone He is faithful and will surly do it.
- We are being changed by this saving relationship we walk in Faith that His Word molds, shapes, and refines our character, to match our His Character. That we mirror His image and likeness.

(Isa 64:8)
8 Yet, O Lord, you are our Father.
We are the clay; you are the potter;
we are all the work of your hand.

- **The character of our FATHER** is good, loving, forgiving, merciful, and peaceable. He is full of grace and patience. He is compassionate, and faithful. He is perfectly, righteous, holy, and pure. He is gentle, comforting, and slow to anger and generous. He is kind and Truthful.

We rest on this next bible verses, as Children of God especially when it comes to matching our Father's Character.

(Matt 19:26) ......, "With man this is impossible, but with God all things are possible."

- It is impossible to form ourselves into the exact imprint of Jesus, this is impossible with man, but with God all things are possible!
- Jesus has all authority, His Kingdom is here, and He reigns forever, as Scripture says, He upholds the universe by the power of His Word.
- His Word testifies to the Character of God and it is our mandate to conform to it.
- This shows us He alone has the power to refine us, shape us, and mold us to His Image and Likeness by the Truth of His Word alone.

"With man this is impossible, but with God all things are possible."

The Characteristics and Identity of a Christian

Co-Labours

Chapter 4

The Characteristics and Identity of a Christian

Co-Labours

Chapter 4

Co-Workers

- Know that we are being separated from the triad which is; the world, Satan, and the sins of our flesh, for God's glory.
- I pray we all are a work in progress, ***As God's <u>co-workers</u>*** we do not receive God's Grace in vain. But we, as professing Christians, must see the necessity of cooperating with the person of the Holy Spirit, in the work at hand, namely, sanctification; that we will be blameless children, set apart for the Father's Glory.
- As co-laborers, we are representatives of God through Christ who is the Chief Federal Head Representative of God.
- We implore to pagans on Christ's behalf "Be reconciled to God," this we do through Jesus Christ and His Gift that He freely shares with us, because He is the only ordained way by the Father to reconcile us, who are lost and dead, in our sins.
- Therefore, He has given us the way by which we come to Him, it is not with sacrifice, it is not with traditions, and it is not by works or merit of our own. But I am not saying it is by no merits or by no works or by no sacrifice do we enter into a saving relationship with the Father. I am just saying it is not of our own sacrifice or traditions, works or merits but of the one qualified to be our Saviour, and Jesus is His name! His sacrifice and traditions, works

and His merits, He freely gives us through Faith as the means to be saved. He loves us dearly and gave Himself for us. He gave His Life, His Body, and His Blood for your relationship with the God of Heaven and earth. "Be reconciled to God our Father today."

(Acts 4:12)
Salvation is found in no one else, for there is no other name under heaven given to men by which we must be saved."

- Therefore, friends, this is a synergistic work of the Holy Spirit. We are ***God's Co-Workers,*** drawing people to Jesus to receive redemption and the Forgiveness of Sin. The People of God will be reconciled to the Father of creation and all Truth, the Father has started a work in us who believe we know this but

  How?

  By the work of the Spirit exposing us to the Truth that the lie is plainly visible and He will bring us to completion, He is faithful and will surely do it, ***"and what we will be has not yet been made known. But we know that when Christ appears, we shall be like him, for we shall see him as he is."***
- Jesus is God with us "Emmanuel" and He is working with us and through us and in us. He is working in us and through us to enable us to succeed in holiness, righteousness, and godliness.

John 5:17-18
17 Jesus said to them, "My Father is always at his work to this very day, and I, too, am working."

(1 Peter 1:13-16 13 Therefore, prepare your minds for action; be self-controlled; set your hope fully on the grace to be given you when Jesus Christ is revealed. 14 As obedient children, do not conform to the evil desires you had when

you lived in ignorance. 15 But just as he who called you is holy, so be holy in all you do; 16 for it is written: "Be holy, because I am holy."

This is the Truth of God's Word!

- We battle the supernatural, we are well aware that the evil one invades our lives moment to moment, but ask yourself this, are we inviting the devil's spirit in are we inviting the spirit that is now working in the sons of disobedience in to work in us and through us?
- Or are we inviting the Holy Spirit of God in, to work in us and through us? What Spirit do you have? The good, loving, gentle, forgiving, merciful, peaceable, gracious, patient, compassionate, faithful, perfect, righteous, holy, pure, slow to anger, Spirit of Truth?
- Because this is the Character of the Father.... And in all we do we must invite His Spirit in.

His Spirit is welcome in my heart, therefore, is His Holy Spirit welcome in yours? I pray, yes!

(Galatians 5:22-24) 22 But the fruit of the Spirit is love, joy, peace, forbearance, kindness, goodness, faithfulness, 23 gentleness and self-control. Against such things there is no law. 24 Those who belong to Christ Jesus have crucified the flesh with its passions and desires.

The Characteristics and Identity of a Christian

Do Not Be Lead Astray

Chapter 5

The Characteristics and Identity of a Christian

Do Not Be Led Astray

Chapter 5

> ***(1 John 3:7-9)[7] Dear children, do not let anyone lead you astray. The one who does what is right is righteous, just as he is righteous. [8] The one who does what is sinful is of the devil, because the devil has been sinning from the beginning. The reason the Son of God appeared was to destroy the devil's work. [9] No one who is born of God will continue to sin, because God's seed remains in them; they cannot go on sinning, because they have been born of God.***

Friends, this text is not meant to discourage us, but to convict the heart of pride. There is a warning here about being led astray by the lie, and we need to see in this chapter what our mandate is as God's Children, to realize that the lie has no share in our lives as Born Again Christians, especially in our worship of the Lord of Glory.

1. ***(1Jn 3:7) Dear children, <u>do not let anyone lead you astray.</u>*** *The one who does what is right is righteous, just as he is righteous.*
   - ***The one who does what is right is righteous, just as he is righteous.*** We will do what is right and righteous just a He does what is right and righteous

How?

- Because being exposed to the Truth of God`s Word is like a tree filling up on nutrients. Therefore, all our hearts must fill themselves with life, the Truth of God`s Word is life.
- It is a necessity for every Born Again Christian to feed on the Truth of God's Word. **Period**! ***That we do not let anyone lead us astray.***

2. [8]***The one who does what is sinful is of the devil, because the devil has been sinning from the beginning. The reason the Son of God appeared was to destroy the devil's work.***

Jesus brought Truth and Grace.

- We all have the Truth of God's Most Holy Word, readily available at ones dispense, found only in the Holy Scriptures.
- Therefore, His Word is Life, reviving the soul.
- So to follow the lie is rebellious and defiant.

Especially when we know the Truth of His Word and proclaim to believe the Truth of His Word.

The Work of Christ

Therefore, the work of Christ is: to reconcile all things to the Father

- So that we can receive sonship and an inheritance in His Kingdom.
- We have been saved from God, by being saved by God, to being saved to God.
- So to see the work of Christ in its end is to see us, who believe reconciled.

We come into the refuge of the Son of God, and we have Faith in the one who made Atonement for our crimes. We have hope in the cross and Him Crucified.

The Devil's Work

The Devil`s work is to destroy our fellowship with the Father, and accuses us to His face, of our guilt, real guilt!

The devil is the accuser and the father of all lies.

- This is ***The reason the Son of God appeared was to destroy the devil's work.***
- Know that the devil hates us and wants us to fall.

  Why?

- Because he knows there is no sin in the presence of Holy God and that sin separates us from our Holy Fellowship we have with Him.
- The devil daily sets a trap, a snare, a pit, and even a net for us to fall into
- He fully enables us to be freely preoccupied in our sin and not exalting, honoring, and worshiping the one who ***appeared to destroy the devil's work*** in our lives.

Jesus offers the blessing of aid, protection, and favor. The devil offers shame, guilt, and regret then he accuses us to the Father

- The Devil tells God we are faithless and disobedient and unworthy of His love. This is his accusation against us, who believe. That we are unworthy sinners.

Presently in this adulterous generation we are sadly exalting honoring and worshiping the lies from the creature, instead of exalting honoring and worshiping the Truth of the Supreme Being.

We are sadly worshiping the creaturely comforts such as vices and materiel possessions instead of the Supreme Being, the one True Invisible and Eternal God.

So the devil is accusing us of real Guilt! His accusations are Truthful.

- However, the evil one is feeding us lies, and the Truth is being suppressed by us, the Children of God.
- This is sad and tragic. But we have hope if we cooperate with the person of the Holy Spirit in every situation, every moment, continually working and exercising our Faith for the Glory of God.
- We give glory to God for we are the workmanship of His hand.
- God always gets the Glory; we should never be ashamed to say the goodness we have came from God.
- Many are doing what they see fit in their own eyes living in half-truth or the lie whatever it is, it is not biblical, but Truth that proceeds from the mouth of man, not God.
- Hence, we are not of God, but ***the one who does what is sinful is of the devil.***

We are becoming the workmanship of the devil's hand not the workmanship of our Father's hand. Sadly,

- We all were in slavery to Satan and oppressed by his rule in this life. Therefore, we have all traded the Truth of God's Word for a lie.
- Not one is completely innocent or without excuse.
- We are as prideful sinners and this is the devil`s work that Jesus will destroy in us and for us.
- This is His Glory saving us, purging us of all indwelling sin, and finally reconciling us to the Father, qualifying us to enter though the gate beautifully dressed in His righteous garments. That He alone clothes us in for this life as His representative, that we shall implore to

pagans "be reconciled to God" this is the ministry of reconciliation, Jesus's ministry IS our ministry.

- The devil's ministry is to create division and enmity between humankind and God that they remain fugitives and children of Wrath. They say "misery loves company" this is the selfishness of the lie of the devil; to see yourself stumble and then causes you brother or sister to fall just so he's not alone.

3. [8] ***The one who does what is sinful is of the devil, because the devil has been sinning from the beginning***

   - We have to remember that ***the devil has been sinning from the beginning*** the devil was sinless, yes! Because in order to be an angel, or better yet, the most beautiful angel of the light, and not only a beautiful angel, but a chief ministry angel of God Almighty. He had to be sinless! **Period!**
   - So the devil knows the Truth of God`s Word much more than you or I do, this is why he knows how to subtly oppose it and by his cunningness, gets us to trade the Truth for the lie.
   - However, one sin and the devil was cast out of heaven, he fell like lighting built from the sky.
   - One sin and the devil was chased away out of the presence of God, all for one sin of pride.

Because he wanted to be worshiped like God.

We see the devil's cunningness in the wilderness when Jesus was tempted by him. This chapter is like a Pilgrimage, a look at the one we exalt, honor, and worship, so that we may not be led astray.

(Matt 4:8-11) 8 Again, the devil took him to a very high mountain and showed him all the kingdoms of the world and their splendor. 9 "All this I will give you," he said, "if you will bow down and worship me." 10 Jesus said to him, "Away

from me, Satan! For it is written: 'Worship the Lord your God, and serve him only."

The devil temps us in the same way,

- We worship Satan every time we surrender and submit our words, actions, and thoughts, or even hand the motives of our hearts over to him.
- We literally bow to him because we believe him and his lies.
- We worship him by believing him and denying the Truth of Our Father's Word.
- We can only have one Lord of our life and ultimately our destiny is in His hands.

Jesus is His Name!

God says ***(Ex 20:3) 3 "You shall have no other gods before me.***

Jesus says: ***'Worship the Lord your God, and serve him only."***

So next time you hear the lie of the devil, think to yourselves: ***"You shall have no other gods before me. 'Worship the Lord your God, and serve him only."***

Next, ask yourselves these question honestly,

- What am I spending my time doing, will it glorify God?
- What am I spending my money on, will it glorify God?
- What am I using my talents for, will it glorify God?

Why am I asking you these questions?

- Because our worship is the energy we spend and the energy we invest our time, talents, and treasures on.
- Because this is where our heart lie's
- Because all we have to do is trace our energy and the investment of our time, talents, and treasures and this is where our worship is.

True biblical worship is,

- reading the bible,
- singing the bible,
- praying the bible,
- preaching the bible,
- studying the bible,
- seeing the bible in the Holy sacraments
- living the culture of the bible
- Being doers of the Word of God EST.

No one who is born of God will continue to sin, because God's seed remains in them; they cannot go on sinning, because they have been born of God.

No one who has the Holy Spirit and has Faith and believes God's Word will continue to sin. That is what this text is saying.

- We know this because the Spirit is Truth, and all Truth comes forth from Him.
- There is no lie in the Truth of God`s Most Word, just as there is no darkness in the light.
- The light is the Spirit realm and the darkness is the devil's domain.
- Therefore, the devil traffics in the darkness of our hearts, with the instrumental cause of pride
- The Holy Spirit traffics in the light of our hearts with the instrumental cause of Faith, Hope, and Love the greatest of these is Love.

Therefore, darkness is the place where we hide and harbour our sins; we hide them from man and from God this is where there is guilt, shame, and regret governing our destiny.

The light is where we expose and reveal our deeds and step into God's presence in humble repentance of our

sin in Faith and love, hope, and peace with the Father is governing our destiny.

- Every born again Christian will do this, we will traffic in and out of darkness and light
- But we must come out of the darkness into the light and we must master over the darkness.
- We worship in Spirit and in Truth as True Children of the Highest we must step into His Light and remain there, and not shift in and out of darkness and light. But No! abide in the light forever. Jesus, asks us to abide in Him and He will abide in us.
- Do we believe this?

That our Father says. ***Luke 15:24 For this son of mine was dead and is alive again; he was lost and is found.' So they began to celebrate.*** We are all the prodigal sons and daughters of our Father.

He loves us and is waiting to celebrate this saving relationship fully with us in His Light!

- **REPENT!** Surrender you hearts to Him, seek Him out, and be intentional in giving Him glory, praise, and thanksgiving, for it is due His Name.

John 4:22-24 [23] Yet a time is coming and has now come when the true worshipers will worship the Father in spirit and truth, for they are the kind of worshipers the Father seeks. [24] God is spirit, and his worshipers must worship in spirit and in truth."

- ***No one who is born of God will continue to sin, because God's seed remains in them; they cannot go on sinning, because they have been born of God.***

This is a necessity, you cannot be born of God and of the devil

- We cannot obey the devil and obey God at the same time.
- We cannot love righteousness and love evil at the same time.
- We cannot have fellowship with the Truth of God's Word and have fellowship with the lies of the devil.

Do we frequently traffic in the domain of darkness or worship in Kingdom of Light? Where is our minds and hearts at? Are they fixed in the worldly realm with the fallen sinful nature or the redemptive realm seated with Christ in the heavenly places? Where is our minds and hearts at when they wonder?

- Are we associating our lives with the carnal life in the sinful flesh, with the desires of our sinful nature, and living in and through our sinful nature?
- Are we living a Spirit filled life, putting on Christ`s nature in the presence of God?
- Are we seeking His Glory?

Friends we can do this by paying special attention to our words, our actions, our thoughts and the motives of our hearts, continually judging them and bringing them under arrest, by making them God Honoring, God Worshiping, and God Glorifying. Amen.

The Characteristics and Identity of a Christian

<u>Equipped</u>

Chapter 6

The Characteristics and Identity of a Christian

Equipped

Chapter 6

Being thoroughly equipped for every good work, for the glory of God

We should be thoroughly equipped for every good work,

Why?

For, the Glory of God.

This is the grace we should be seeking for, asking for, and knock on the door for, that our Father's Holy Name is vindicated and that He gets the Glory for His people who manifest His Son Jesus Christ and flesh Him out in this fallen world. That God would get the Glory in the workmanship of His hands for He will equip every one of us,

- His people
- His adopted children
- His special and common vessels,
- His instruments

who are saved by His Grace, through Faith, in His Son Jesus Christ, alone.

Therefore, just stop and think of it. If I said that a Christian does not gratify the desires of their flesh and they do not seek instant gratification in lust, but instead they seek long term joy in the Lord, in that they will enjoy Him forever as their main priority.

I would say that this Christian is separate from the world, but as we see the Christian characteristics should be very, very, different from the world. But in most churches, the professing Christian is not distinguished as different from non-believers, this is sad friends. Therefore, are we holy and set apart from the world and the popularity of its allure?

(1 John 2:15-17) [15] ***Do not love the world or the things in the world. If anyone loves the world, the love of the Father is not in him.*** [16] ***For all that is in the world—the desires of the flesh and the desires of the eyes and pride of life—is not from the Father but is from the world.*** [17] ***And the world is passing away along with its desires, but whoever does the will of God abides forever.***

Our Father is Holy; we must be holy as He is Holy: set apart for His Glory.

> ***(1 Thessalonians 4:3-5)*** [3] ***For this is the will of God, your sanctification: that you should abstain from sexual immorality;*** [4] ***that each of you should know how to possess his own vessel in sanctification and honor,*** [5] ***not in passion of lust, like the Gentiles who do not know God;***
>
> *"[5] not in passion of lust, like the Gentiles who do not know God;"*

In all, our words, our actions, and our thoughts, and even the motives of our hearts must come into alignment with our Father's

words,

actions,

thoughts,

and motives of His heart, that His will be done: our Sanctification.

Namely, we follow and act and speak as Jesus did; who is the perfect imprint of God's Glorified Character. We are not to seek the flesh and its desires. Instead, we seek the Holy Spirit and the Truth, because seeking the Truth will enable us to reject the lie, we will faithfully walk in the refuge of our Lord and Saviour, Jesus Christ and abide in the TRUTH.

This is His Hope for us, that you remain in the Truth and reject the lie we are sanctified by the Word and the God's Word is the Truth.

> ***(Galatians 5:19-21)[19] The acts of the flesh are obvious: sexual immorality, impurity and debauchery; [20] idolatry and witchcraft; hatred, discord, jealousy, fits of rage, selfish ambition, dissensions, factions [21] and envy; drunkenness, orgies, and the like. I warn you, as I did before, that those who live like this will not inherit the kingdom of God.***

This remark is not applying only to the world. ***I warn you, as I did before, that those who live like this will not inherit the kingdom of God.***

Why?

- Because the believers who have been redeemed and saved, even freed from slavery to sin, still want pleasure now!
- Therefore, when our desire is to be an instrument of love who draws people to God and bring our Father glory, we will begin to mortify sin, and forsake our way and adopt the Father's way. His way is for us to replicate His Son, and honor His Son, and exalt His Son, and we worship His Son, and live through His Son through the Instrumental Cause of Faith.
- Therefore, when our desire is to be an instrument of sin and evil that brings our Father dishonor, we will begin to embrace sin, and cling to our ways and forsake the Father's way. This is the devil's will that we replicate the

fallen world around us, our own sinful flesh and ultimately the devil himself, he desires us to honor him, and exalt him, and worship him and live through him through the instrumental cause of pride, arrogance, selfishness, and rebellion, against The One True God.

This struggle I am talking about is not for today only or for one category of people, but for the whole of humanity throughout time.

(Romans 6:12-14)[12] Therefore do not let sin reign in your mortal body so that you obey its evil desires. [13] Do not offer any part of yourself to sin as an instrument of wickedness, but rather offer yourselves to God as those who have been brought from death to life; and offer every part of yourself to him as an instrument of righteousness. [14] For sin shall no longer be your master, because you are not under the law, but under grace.

Therefore, anything that stops us from enjoying fellowship with our Father is a sin.

Sin is an offence and transgression against us personally if we love our Father.

Why?

Because when our character conforms to His Character everything that opposes His Character, opposes our character. In addition, everything that threatens His Character, threatens ours. If we are His Children our response is to give Him all that is due His Name.

- Sin is a defilement of the integrity of the Truth of God's Word.
- When God says no and we proceed regardless, we trade the Truth of God's Word for a lie. This is the heart of pride.
- When we exult ourselves above God's Authority, we are literally embracing pride, and the devil wins.

This is tragic and we are in shambles, especially when we see the price His Son paid for reconciling us to the Father: The Good, loving, gentle, forgiving, merciful, peaceable, gracious, patient, compassionate, faithful, perfect, righteous, holy, pure, slow to anger, Father that we love and adore.

Sin is not only destructive but not how we love our Father

- Sin is not only destructive, but we know that sin is not how we love our Father, but how we oppose Him. Sin intensely stops our spiritual growth.

Why?

Because it stops us from changing, replicating, demonstrating, and advocating the Father's Character to His Creation and drawing them to Jesus the Son, to receive His Gift.

- We are His Children we are His Representatives, with His Promised Holy Spirit; we glorify Him and worship Him, for He is Worthy and Exalted above all creation. Our Father is Holy; we must be holy as He is Holy: set apart for His Glory.
- We, as professing Christians, must see the necessity of cooperating with the person of the Holy Spirit in the work of sanctification; that we will be blameless children, set apart for the Father's glory. There are no chains of bondage and grip of debauchery that His Love can't break. We do not need self-reliance, we need God Dependency, we need His Spirit

The Holy Spirit directs us to the Truth

- We love the Truth;
- We do not hide from the Truth.
- We embrace the Truth,
- We support the Truth,
- We are forthcoming with the Truth,
- We uphold the Truth,

- We defend the Truth,
- And if need be, we would die for the Truth

Debauchery and sexual immorality ought to be very, very, very far from us.

Why?

Because our sin was once housed in our hearts, but now, through our regeneration and renewal of our minds, we have been transformed and restored though our rebirth. The Holy Spirit is housed in us if we abide. Our hearts have had a quickening change; through our rebirth we have vacated our old ways and have adopted Christ's Way; instead of rejecting the Truth that gives us life, we embrace the Holy Spirit of Truth with gladness. We embrace the Truth even if we suffer on account of it.

Why?

For it is better to suffer for righteousness' sake instead of for sin's sake.

Why?

Because if we have no share in the suffering of Christ for righteousness' sake, then we have no share in Christ, in His life, death and resurrection. This is the first element we have to grasp in the process of becoming equipped for the pilgrimage that lay before us as abiding disciples of Jesus which is, that we will all suffer no matter what. However, the children of God ought to be equipped and know our suffering is for Christ's sake not for the devil's sake.

The Characteristics and Identity of a Christian

Fight Sin

Chapter 7

The Characteristics and Identity of a Christian

Fight Sin

Chapter 7

This fallen corrupt life is all we have ever known, so to forsake our way and adopt Christ's Way is virtually impossible. We have to have the continual filling of the Holy Spirit, we need supernatural heart surgery, this is a work of Grace from the Father's Word of Truth that commanded the light and has all capability to heal the heart.

We need to turn from our sin, this is what it means to repent. However, we need to have a willing heart in order to change like a child receiving sound instruction, that heart then has the power to bind the conscience. We grow by His Grace which is everything undeserved that comes down from our Father's hands, only God can change the hearts' desires so.

The first elements to fighting sin is:

- to persistently pray for the heart to change
- the willingness to give full control of our will to Him in all situations, circumstances, and the present moment
- actively seek Him out in all areas of your life

So what can we do?

Well to start, we need a willing heart to submit and surrender every situation or circumstance, as well as the present moment over to our Lord and Saviour's care and attention.

- He is tender towards those who depend on Him
- He is tender towards those who rely on Him
- He is tender towards those who seek Him

We get to Desire the things He desires, to love the things He loves, and to hate the things He hates, if need be, flee from the things He flees from.

Therefore, it is plain to see that all of humankind has an appetite for the desires of sin.

- Sadly, we have total depravity: the things we want to do, we do not do because we are in bondage and slavery to our sins and vices
- We have all fallen into a pit, been caught in the snare, walked into a trap, or even been carried away in a net.
- "Help" we cry out to the Lord

You know and I know "Help!" is the very first prayer we ever prayed! So, for us to think we can fight sin on our own, we are plainly deceiving ourselves.

Jesus is our only Hope, we are too weak. When we are weak, He is strong.

- We just need to believe in His Power to defend us.
- We just need to believe in His Power to help us.
- We just need to believe in His Power to strengthen us.
- We just need to believe in His Power to restore us.
- We just need to believe in His Power to save us.

The nature of the pit, the snare, the trap, or net, is usually a visible thing in this fallen world, these are the things that the evil one offers to our fallen nature; that sadly we receive with open arms.

Why?

- Because we trade the Truth of God's Word for a lie

- The things we receive from the triad are evil, but they are subtle in their offering them to us, masquerading as light
- We know that the world, the devil, and the sinful flesh are fallen and corrupted
- Everything they offer us is in place of what our Heavenly Father has stored up for His people in eternity past.
- The Father has stored up for us His Favor, His Aid, and His Protection; ultimately His Sovereign Blessings that can never be measured or counted.
- Thus, the triad actually opposes our Father's Good and Perfect Nature to bless us, as His Children.

I believe biblically this is why every professing Christian must be conscious and discerning to see the end of everything, to judge everything. Therefore, every choice we make has a consequence. The Christian who is fighting sin first needs to distinguish good from evil and be very vigilant in his or her choices that are heaven bound and reject those that are hell bound.

- Either we chose the Truth or the lie!
- One gives life, love, hope, and peace
- While the other breeds death, guilt, regret and shame.

We must even distinguish the spirit that is in us.

- Do we have a disobedient spirit or and carnal spirit?
- Do we have the Holy Spirit full of fire, passion, and zeal for the expansion of His Kingdom?
- Is our spirit lukewarm and quenched?
- Or is the spirit we have hot, pressed down, shaken up, and overflowing in joy?
- Never ever quench the Spirit of our Lord Jesus Christ.

(Romans 8:12-17) [12] Therefore, brethren, we are debtors—not to the flesh, to live according to the flesh. [13] For if you live according to the flesh you will die; but if by the Spirit you put to death the deeds of the body, you will live. [14] For as many as are led by the Spirit of God, these are sons of God.

[15] For you did not receive the spirit of bondage again to fear, but you received the Spirit of adoption by whom we cry out, "Abba, Father." [16] The Spirit Himself bears witness with our spirit that we are children of God, [17] and if children, then heirs—heirs of God and joint heirs with Christ, if indeed we suffer with Him, that we may also be glorified together.

The Scriptures are a lamp to our feet along the narrow path to life, but know this, that along this path the flesh is easily blinded by the allure of this world that is filled to the brim with people with sinful nature. The presence of sin remains always, but we ought to co-labour with the Spirit of God to purge all indwelling sin, and "Cleanse the inside of the cup!"

When we are led into a pit, a snare, a trap and a net, this is where we fall into sin and are helpless to escape.

- Each of us has fallen in to a pit, snare, and trap or even been caught in a net.
- No one is exempt from this calamity.
- However, one season to the next there are always new trials for the children of God; if we are not careful and vigilant, we can fall into a pit, a snare, a trap or a net, for a season

Why?

- Because if we are not careful and vigilant we will not be on guard and awake, but blinded and sleeping.

(Matthew 6:33)[33] But seek first the kingdom of God and His righteousness, and all these things shall be added to you.

Know this friends,

- If we are not careful and vigilant we can still gratify the desires of our flesh,
- If we are not careful and vigilant we can follow after the popularity of the world and trade the Truth for a lie,

- And if we are not careful and vigilant we can still hear the subtle call of the evil one drawing us to the desires that dishonor our Father.
- Remember the lamp for our feet is God's Most Holy Word, and His Word is the Truth and the very source that sets us free.
- For God's Word has the power to fill any amount of spiritual ignorance with the light and enlightenment of His Objective Truth and His Objective Reality that He presents to us, to believe in this Life.

John 14:6-7
6 Jesus answered, "I am the way and the truth and the life. No one comes to the Father except through me. 7 If you really knew me, you would know my Father as well. From now on, you do know him and have seen him."

Therefore, all men and women and children can fall into a pit: this is our debauchery and our slavery to Satan and sin. Therefore, we have been freed from the slavery of Satan and sin, as Christians, but can slip back into sin still.

- Because the presence still remains
- Because the allure still remains
- Because the indwelt sin in us still remains

Why?

Because we our selves have fallen into the pit, and some jump in the pit, our lack of wisdom and decrement to distinguish good from evil is our down fall. But the inability to choose good over evil is our fallen plight.

- We are reckless
- We are rebellious
- We are defiant

We can choose the color of shirt we want to wear, but to stop practicing a vice or a sin; the will is in bondage and will not submit to God.

We all need The Savior

- We all need Jesus to liberate us and deliver us out of the hands of the enemy.
- We all need salvation from the oppression of sin.
- We all have the law written on our hearts so have we are without excuse, saints.
- We are without excuses!
- We all know the good from the bad
- We all know our enemy.

May it never be that any saint commit treason against God and conform to the enemy while professing love to the Father, the Son, and Holy Spirit, and yet pledges allegiance to Satan in a revolt against the One True God and His Kingdom. May it never be!

The Characteristics and Identity of a Christian

Freed

Chapter 8

The Characteristics and Identity of a Christian

Freed

Chapter 8

We are born of God, and sin opposes Him, therefore, this is our dilemma as sinners our life is a struggle back and forward in and out of darkness and light. Even though we are saved by grace and freed from the bondage of Satan, and we know the Truth of God's Word, even further, His law is written on our hearts causing us to obey His Statuses and Precepts. Even further, we know that He has set us free, but the presence of the lie remains.

Like putting a drop of cyanide in a glass of water, the lie of Satan has permeated through the whole substance, this is the lie of the devil in our contingent, derived, and finite fallen world, the lie always remains.

- The lie remains, because the devil is not fully destroyed yet, but is in chains.
- He cannot attack us, but he can still lure us into the lie and tempt us with the lie that opposes our Father's Truth that He freely gives us.
- We do not first study the lie and teaching of it, but study the Word of God and know it to defend ourselves boldly against the lie.
- We study the Word of God to know the counterfeit, if we know the Word of God, then we can easily tell when the devil is teaching us false doctrine or when the cunningness and subtleness and the persistence of the devil counterfeits the Truth.

- We do this so that when the lie comes to put us in bondage, we can fight and not embrace the lie and make it a stronghold against the devil in our lives.
- When the devil gets us to trade the Truth for the lie, we lose and he wins the battle. How tragic and devastating.
- But when we reject the lie and run to the Truth, who is Christ, and embrace Him, we win God's favor!

(John 8:34-36)
34 Jesus replied, "I tell you the truth, everyone who sins is a slave to sin. 35 Now a slave has no permanent place in the family, but a son belongs to it forever. 36 So if the Son sets you free, you will be free indeed

This is the essence of our hope in conforming to Jesus, ***36 So if the Son sets you free, you will be free indeed*** that God's seed remains in us, and we abide, that His Word remains in us every day we wake, and Jesus is there always leading us to the Truth.

- The Faith He gives us from His Word, is penetrating the hardness of our heart, and exposing us to the Truth of the Father`s Love for us if we abide.
- His Word is working in us and through us; moment by moment if we abide.
- The Father is showing us the right and righteous path to walk in His Most Holy Word if we abide.

His Word is the lamp to our feet, so we do not fall into a pit, a snare, and trap, or be carried away in a net. Therefore, we are in the redemptive realm, we are in the Kingdom of God, eternity has been put in our hearts. He has given full authority to His Son. His Son has Supreme Authority, so as Born Again Christians, our only hope is that God has freed us completely from the bondage and debauchery of sin even though sin is in the world. In dwelling sin is being purged from the Children of God. Therefore, Father God is doing the work in us; shaping us, molding us into the imprint of His Son. Amen

Phil 1:5-6 Reads

- ***6 being confident of this, that he who began a good work in you will carry it on to completion until the day of Christ Jesus.***

Michelangelo made the awesome sculpture of King David the grandest and most intricate sculpture he carved, He delicately carved it with a chisel and hammer. Thus, after it was done people were amazed and looked at it with awe, they asked him, "How did you ever finish this magnificent sculpture of King David." You know what he said:

"I just took away everything that was not David."

This is exactly what our Father is doing with us. He is taking away everything that is not His Son's

- Nature
- Likeness
- Image
- Character

As we are pressing into the mold of Jesus, our pride and sin is being taken away, and in the end the

- **Nature**
- **Likeness**
- **Image**
- **Character of Jesus will be left in us who believe.**

Therefore, we will be Christ-like, for we shall see Him as He is and we will behold His Glory and the richness of His Glory will shine on us forever.

Phil 1:5-6

6 being confident of this, that he who began a good work in you will carry it on to completion until the day of Christ Jesus.

The Characteristics and Identity of a Christian

Holiness

Chapter 9

The Characteristics and Identity of a Christian

Holiness

Chapter 9

The Sanctification of Christ, is the Christian Character.

- This chapter of holiness is about the Christian Character, not necessarily the origin of salvation. Therefore, we know that Justification is one part of salvation, but all who are justified are glorified; ***those he justified, he also glorified.*** The basic accent of the New Testament is a Call to Sanctification. This is the Revealed Will of God for you and for me, as professing Christians.

(1 Thess 4:3-4)
It is God's will that you should be sanctified: that you should avoid sexual immorality; 4 that each of you should learn to control his own body in a way that is holy and honorable,

- Thus, all True Christians will grow in Christ, this is a part of Jesus' High Priestly Prayer. When He made Intercessory Prayer for His Disciples and on behalf of all those who would believe, it was his intention to Sanctify us by The Truth.

(John 17:17-23)
17 Sanctify them by the truth; your word is truth.
18 As you sent me into the world, I have sent them into the world. 19 For them I sanctify myself, that they too may be truly sanctified.

20 "My prayer is not for them alone. I pray also for those who will believe in me through their message,

Next the Lord prays that we would be one with Him,

- This shows the unity the Father, the Son, and the Holy Spirit.
- This is the unity of the Trinity
- Jesus is praying to the Father that our salvation would come to pass
- This salvation was declared to the prophets and the psalmists that God would send a Saviour to Israel.

And He did!

John 1:10-13
10 He was in the world, and though the world was made through him, the world did not recognize him. [11] He came to that which was his own, but his own did not receive him. [12] Yet to all who received him, to those who believed in his name, he gave the right to become children of God— [13] children born not of natural descent, nor of human decision or a husband's will, but born of God.

Christian's Struggle

Not one Christian's sin more to gain more grace. But as Christians we push and press into the kingdom.

- We struggle to produce the fruits of the Spirit
- We struggle to be intentional in sharing the good news
- We struggle in the battle of turning from sin

So we pray hard that we will receive more and more grace to obey and to be enabled to not sin, but to turn from our sin and any thing that offends our Father's Holiness!

This is Amazing Grace!

- This is the work of the person of the Holy Spirit, leading us to everything pleasing to the Father,
- Teaching us by exposing us to the Truth of God's Word.
- Thus, the Truth binds the conscience.
- To be exposed to the Truth, one will believe and have Faith in the one from which it comes or reject it!

Brothers and Sisters

- Obey the Word
- Submit to the Word
- Fall under the Lordship of the Word who is Christ Jesus, the logos, the Word made flesh.

Thus, by the Power of His Holy Word

- He upholds the universe by His grace and Truth
- To all who are hungry and thirsty He offers His Grace and Truth
- He gives them the free right to drink and eat of His Grace and Truth
- He is our King Holy, Holy, Holy

Jesus gets the glory in the Father's Work, we as co-labours get to be exposed to the radiation of God's Glory and His Holiness.

- All disorder in our thinking He makes it come into order, He is continually renewing our mind by the Truth of His Word
- He gives us the ability to turn from everything that displeases Him and His Holiness, by binding our conscience with The Truth.

Your belief starts the moment that the Authority of God's Word is paramount in your life!

God will show us

- That we need to trust Him
- That we need to have Faith in Him
- That we need to believe that He is faithful
- That we need to see that He is perfectly Holy
- That we need to adopt His Son's Character
- That we need seek out the Christian Character
- That we need to bear the mark of faithfulness and holiness

Because we are Children of God and He is purely faithful and Holy, Holy, Holy.

This is the Christian character

This is the Christian character: being <u>disciplined</u> in the <u>struggle</u> to conform to the Image, Likeness, Nature and Character of Jesus Christ, who is the Perfect Imprint of the Father.

(1 Peter 1:13-16) Be Holy [13] Therefore, with minds that are alert and fully sober, set your hope on the grace to be brought to you when Jesus Christ is revealed at his coming. [14] As obedient children, do not conform to the evil desires you had when you lived in ignorance. [15] But just as he who called you is holy, so be holy in all you do; [16] for it is written: "Be holy, because I am holy."

This struggle for holiness is not easy;

- The narrow road is not the broad road, and the broad road is not the narrow road.
- Few follow the narrow road, but many follow the broad road.

Why?

- Because the broad road appeals to our desires, whereas the narrow road is a stumbling block of offence to many.

We are to pick up our cross, and deny our flesh, and follow Jesus; this is not the easy road but the hard road, and few follow

- Know this, that the narrow road is the road that is holy and is heaven bound
- The broad road is corrupt and this road is hell bound.

(Hebrews 12:12-13)[12] Therefore, strengthen your feeble arms and weak knees. [13] "Make level paths for your feet," so that the lame may not be disabled, but rather healed. Make every effort to live in peace with everyone and to be holy; without holiness no one will see the Lord.

Struggle for God's Glory

We as Christians are in for a struggle,

- Spiritual growth is a struggle
- Achieving holiness is a struggle
- Conforming to Jesus is a struggle

But friends, undeserved forgiveness is not a Christian struggle, it is not achieving or conforming to what God has set before humankind to attain, nor is it the righteous path to walk in.

We should be seeking the latter such as:

- Undeserved spiritual gifts,
- Undeserved fruits of the Spirit,
- Undeserved sanctification
- Undeserved consecration
- Undeserved filling of the Holy Spirit,
- Undeserved authentic righteousness,
- Undeserved salvation,
- Undeserved kindness,

Dear friends, as we see in this list, all we have to do is put underserved in front of these words and it is grace.

Even our breath is by God's Grace.

Think about it, what grace are you receiving right now?

- Even our breath is undeserved in light of our sin, "We are all getting way better than we do deserve, are we not?"

Our Father is gracious and loving and does not want to see any of us perish in ruin, this is His Hope, that we forsake our corrupt conduct and adopt His Holy Conduct.

Holiness
Godliness
Righteousness

- His hope is that we succeed in holiness, godliness, and righteousness and He loves seeing His Children's potential grow in these practises
- His hope is that we all have a share in His Holiness, His Godliness, and His Righteousness. He loves seeing His Children's potential grow in these practises
- His hope is that we all receive share of His Glory, as the Workmanship of His Hands on the Final Day of Judgment, when Christ will come to gather His Elect

The Characteristics and Identity of a Christian

Preparedness

Chapter 10

The Characteristics and Identity of a Christian

Preparedness

Chapter 10

The pit is a dark and scary place for anyone.

Why?

Because we feel helpless to escape. We need more than prayers, more than food and clothing. What we need is the Saviour, we need to be liberated from the confines of the pit! So we can come on level ground and be free from the bondage of sin. We have all fallen and it's the devil's oppression that does not release us from our sin, but confines us in our sin, even to the point of utter helplessness. We all need to be set free from our sins, this is the work we ought to participate in and practice diligently in the process of cleansing us from all indwelling sin, I have been talking about cleaning the inside of the cup this is a Christian's main priority to submit to Jesus and allow Him to cleanse us from all indwelling sin; we need our Saviour Jesus to free us, and to deliver us out of the pit.

However, it is like a man that walked into a pit and he was stranded but could not reach the top, he could see the top of the pit, but nothing beyond.

- He was seeking help everywhere by all means
- Ultimately he was groping around in the dark with
    - No hope
    - No light

- No one to help Him
- No one to save Him
- No one to deliver Him out of the confines of the pit.

Then, out of nowhere the Lord appeared and helped him in his helplessness. Thus,

He is the Way,

the Truth,

and the Life.

What this means is we follow Jesus's way

- We submit ourselves
- We surrender ourselves
- We humble ourselves
- And we obey

The most used phrase from a Christian ought to be, "Yes! Lord, may Your Will be done."

The most common Christian Characteristic should be Preparedness, and by grabbing the rope He has let down for us to grab, we trust Him to pull us up to safety, and deliver us out of the confines of our sin. We cannot see Him, but we know He is there always.

This is the Christian Life we live:

- Under the Authority of God
- In the Presence of God
- To the Glory and Honor of God

Our sin in the pit becomes overdeveloped easily; it is not getting better, but worse. In addition, every human will go through this. Therefore, the things we once said we would never do, now we are doing them, and not only doing them, but doing much more than we ever said we would ever do.

For the heart is not happy with wholesome things any longer at this stage, but our appetites have become more perverse, evil, defiling, and unclean, our lesser sins have grown into an over developed deformity of moral breach. For example, we once thought it was okay to look at missionary position on the porn site. Then, we needed more perverse things, because our appetite had a hunger for more perverse substances. We are an adulterous generation.

We should not be down for the count against sin but we, as Christians, must be **down for the cause**, by being against sin: this is the Synergistic Work of God, in the Born Again Christians. Believing the Truth of God's Word then demonstrate it, is like saying do not preach Truth, Love and Grace of God only, but demonstrate the Truth, Love and Grace of God boldly.

We see in the pit that the walls are easily breached; I am saying that the integrity of God's Law is overtaken and there is no defence against the enemy. Sadly, there is no opposition to the enemy, but a spirit of lax and conformity to the enemy is evident in this rebellious and adulterous generation. This is sad friends. Have we, as a society, forgotten the Saving Power of the Saviour?

Mark 8:38
If anyone is ashamed of me and my words in this adulterous and sinful generation, the Son of Man will be ashamed of him when he comes in his Father's glory with the holy angels."

The heart is easily willing to cave into the enemy and believe its lies, this is the enemies', stronghold: the manifestation of the lie. Brother & Sisters, this is High Treason punishable by death in the Court of Canada. Conforming to the enemy is a Capital Offence. Why are we so easily sympathetic toward sin? For it is High Treason against Holy God, and a revolt against

Him and His Lordship, not only Treason to the one we worship and praise, but to our Dear Father in Heaven who is Blameless and Innocent.

(Romans 12:1-4) I beseech you therefore, brethren, by the mercies of God, that you present your bodies a living sacrifice, holy, acceptable to God, which is your reasonable service. [2] And do not be conformed to this world, but be transformed by the renewing of your mind, that you may prove what is that good and acceptable and perfect will of God.

Therefore, we as Christian's should hate sin, because we are not weak

- We have the Power of God dwelling in us
- We have the Holy Spirit that continually seeks after the Love of the Father
- We will enjoy His Love forever

We will conform to His Son's Likeness, Image, Nature, and Character. The disobedient spirit lacks in self-control and is unwilling to submit to the Lordship of Christ and produce the Fruits of the Spirit, which ultimately, is the very Character of Jesus.

In addition, the Law of God has been written on all of our hearts. For many, not few, but many professing Christians, this wall of morality and integrity and character are more than breached, they are falling and crumbling down all around us in the church. Whether it is visible or invisible we must know that ruin is always visible to God, for He alone knows our heart's condition and what we truly value in our lives.

(Psalm 51:6-10)[6] Behold, you desire truth in the inward parts, and in the hidden part You will make me to know wisdom.[7] Purge me with hyssop, and I shall be clean; Wash me, and I shall be whiter than snow.[8] Make me hear joy and gladness, That the bones You have broken may rejoice.[9] Hide Your

face from my sins, and blot out all my iniquities.[10] Create in me a clean heart, O God, and renew a steadfast spirit within

Ask yourself this:

What spirit is dwelling in you?

- What values do you hold closest to your heart?
- Do you have the Holy Spirit of Truth and Life, or do you have the disobedient spirit of death?
- Truth with a capital T is scarce. However, self-control, is the scarcest fruit on the vine in this generation.
- And relativism is ramped; a lie we have traded for the Truth of God's Word
- Humanity sees fit, in their own eyes, the Truth of God's Word traded for the lies of the devil. We see in Scripture that this very practice goes back to Genesis Chapter 3, this is carried on to text generation to the first sin of murder by Cain to his own brother Abel.

(Genesis 4:7)[7] If you do well, will you not be accepted? And if you do not do well, sin lies at the door. And its desire is for you, but you should rule over it.

Thus, in light there is no dark, because what fellowship does darkness have with light?

- None!
- Sin stops us from being blessed;
- The blessings that our Father has stored up for us, in our active rebellion, are waiting for us right now!
- God in His Long-Suffering, desires to pour these blessing out on His People. But if we do bad, shall we receive good?
- Absolutely not!

(Genesis 4:6-7)[6] So the LORD said to Cain, "Why are you angry? And why has your countenance fallen? [7] If you do well, will you not be accepted? And if you do not do well, sin lies at the door. And its desire is for you, but you should rule over it."

Do not be deceived. We receive nothing from God's Surplus of His blessings that He has stored up for His people, if we do not

Abide in Him,

and Follow Him,

and Live like He Did!

If you do well, will you not be accepted?! We have no share with Him if we are outside His Will. Our sanctification is inside His Will; it is inside every human's duty to abstain from the practice of sin. So seek the Kingdom first and His Righteousness and everything shall be added on to you.

We must have preparedness and be ready for the war against sin that lays before us in our Christian pilgrimage.

The trap that was laid for "us" was not seen by "us" because the trap was not expected, or anticipated, however, it abruptly sprang, to our dismay, with all intentions, for our utter ruin as a professing Christian. The net that has fallen over us, is silent, but deadly, it entangles us and we are caught in the entrapment of it and then we are dragged away into sin.

But God being rich in mercy sees us in our helpless state

- His mighty hand reaches out for us
- He frees us from the bondage of sin
- He delivers us from slavery to Satan
- He protects us
- He guards us
- He ministers to us through the Spirit of Love
- The Truth of God's Word has set us free
- The Lord softly places us back on the path
- We are heaven bound
- He has set us on His Path to Eternal Life

As we carry on the long Pilgrimage that lays ahead of us, to His heaven we have all hope.

This is why we need to be vigilant and cautious brothers and sisters.

This is the Christian Character: Preparedness.

Preparedness: dictionary.com
/prɪˈpɛərɪdnɪs/ noun

1. the state of being prepared or ready, esp militarily ready for war

Psalm 28:1-2
28 ***To you, O LORD, I call;***
my rock, be not deaf to me,
lest, if you be silent to me,
I become like those who go down to the pit.
[2] ***Hear the voice of my pleas for mercy,***
when I cry to you for help,
when I lift up my hands
toward your most holy sanctuary.

We, as professing Christians, have to be at war on three different fronts. To think that this will be easy or to say it is easy and that there is no threat would be a ghastly lie!

Why?

Because it will be very hard to have war on three different fronts, for a lifetime.

- It will not be a battle that you can be lax in.
- Furthermore, it is moment to moment, that this battle takes place
- Everyday and everywhere you go, it is all around us as Christians.
- We have the mind of Christ and the Spirit of God, so this battle is visible to us.

- We have the law written on our hearts, and above all God causes us to walk in His Precepts and Status.

See, our Christian Character, is under assault from the enemy

- Hour to hour
- Minute to minute
- Day to day
- Week to week,

Our enemy is not one fold, we brothers and sisters, oppose three enemies that each have their own artillery.

- They are fueled by murder and lies

***(James 4:7-8)* [7] *Submit yourselves therefore to God. Resist the devil, and he will flee from you.* [8] *Draw near to God, and he will draw near to you. Cleanse your hands, you sinners, and purify your hearts, you double-minded.* [9]**

Our distinct opposition is not distinct to one threat, like when one country is opposed to another, but no! We are opposing three fold and these three are one in the same purpose, plan, and will, however, distinct in artillery:

- Like a fighter plane,
- Like a tank,
- Like a soldier is distinct in combated in their vehicles.

When they initiate war, they have the same purposes, plan, and will, but are distinct in artillery:

Therefore, they want to destroy our Fellowship we have with the Father, the Son, and the Holy Spirit and send us into:

- Despair
- Confusion
- Self-reliance

- Pride
- Ego
- Arrogance
- Eternal ruin

(1 Peter 5:8-9)[8] ***Be sober-minded; be watchful. Your adversary the devil prowls around like a roaring lion, seeking someone to devour.*** [9] ***Resist him, firm in your faith, knowing that the same kinds of suffering are being experienced by your brotherhood throughout the world.***

The triad wants us to adopt their character and forsake our Fathers. They want to weaken our Identity in Christ and lead us into confusion, that we not be drawn to Christ but are fugitives to Him. The triad's plan is to defile the integrity, identity, and character of the Children of God and to deface His Holiness to all. They do so by defiling God's Own Children before all, in so that they commit treason and partake in the devil's revolt against God, by conforming us to the enemy's:

- Image
- Likeness
- Nature
- Character

The triad's Purpose is to destroy God's Workmanship in the glorification of His Precious Children.

The triad's will, is bent on pushing us into ruin, not only ruin, but eternal ruin; forever. In that, we as God's Children are washed away in the lies of the pit, the snare, the trap, and the net, never to be found or rescued.

Keep your eyes open because the war is all around us,

- Love one another
- Be perfect representatives of God's Character by reflecting His Perfect Character to the fallen world around us

Know that we are all either on the offensive or defensive side, everyone is a part of this war. Dear friends, seek out the Saviour and the one who has Sovereign Authority in the earthly and spiritual realm over Satan, sin, and death.

Jesus is His Name.

This preparedness that we have looked at will only be effective when we submit and surrender our life to the Lordship of Jesus Christ.

- To the one who has Authority over the enemy
- To the one who can over take the enemy
- To the one who can destroy the enemy

The Characteristics and Identity of a Christian

The Truth

Chapter 11

The Characteristics and Identity of a Christian

The Truth

Chapter 11

We as professing Christians, should be the most aware of the Truth of God's Word in our lives, we need to know that as God's Children, the Truth of His Word is written on our hearts. ***(Duet 30:14) No, the word is very near you; it is in your mouth and in your heart so you may obey it.*** In this chapter we will look at The Truth, that we were brought forth in The Word, and we have been Born Again by The Most:

- Holy
- Sacred
- Sanctified
- Consecrated
- And Special Word

We know the Truth of God's Word. He is working in us and through us, and for His Glory by making us more like His Son. God is Praiseworthy and Honor is due His Name.

(1 Peter 1:23-25)
23 For you have been born again, not of perishable seed, <u>but of imperishable, through the living and enduring word of God.</u> 24 For,
"All men are like grass,
and all their glory is like the flowers of the field;
the grass withers and the flowers fall,
25 but the word of the Lord stands forever."
And this is the word that was preached to you.

Know that we are a work in progress; Period!

- We all are in different places in our sanctification
- When we look back five years we can easily see our transformation
- Day to day it seems like we are moving in turtle speed in our spiritual growth, but over many seasons, the Truth of God's Word becomes evident in our lives
- Our Faith becomes established and rooted and grounded in Christ who abundantly supplies the Truth and the Grace that transforms us

(Titus 3:4-6) 4 But when the kindness and love of God our Savior appeared, 5 he saved us, not because of righteous things we had done, but because of his mercy. He saved us through the washing of rebirth and renewal by the Holy Spirit, 6 whom he poured out on us generously through Jesus Christ our Savior,

We are born again Children of the Father of Truth and Grace. We will, abandon pride and adopt humility, because the teaching of God's Word will bind our conscience with The Truth.

- We will not hate anyone; but love and forgive, even our enemies
- We will even forsake our fallen likeness, image, nature, and character; and we will adopt our Father's Likeness, Image, Nature, and Character and every knee will bow
- Adopting the Father's Desires, Passions and Love, we can adopt His Purpose, Plan, and Will
- We get to even have the chance to adopt His Values
- We can adopt His Moral and Ethical Law
- His Word supplies all this and much, much more
- God's Word even supplies the principles to apply wisdom, knowledge, and understanding to one's life and all that pertains to God's Likeness, Image, Nature and Character that we can share in His Identity.

God's Word Is:

- Teaching us
- Reproofing us
- Correcting us
- Training us
- Instructing us

We will seek the Father's Glory!

The enabling power of the Holy Spirit will give us the heart and courage to adopt Jesus': Temperament, Nature, Personality, Disposition, Image and Likeness, His Self, and His Traits, His Moral and Ethical Qualities, His Reputation, Behaviour, and Conduct, even His Nature. that is found only in the Truth of God's Word.

Our identity is in Christ, our image is in Christ, and so shouldn't our character be in Christ as well?

Why?

- That we may live life more abundantly, now!
- Live in peace with God more closely now!
- And know the Fatherhood of God more intimately now!
- To share in the character of the Father to be more holy now!

We are the workmanship of the Father, so shouldn`t our characters come into alignment with our Father's Character?

- That our heart be His Heart
- That our desires be His Desires
- That our passions be His Passions
- That our love be His Love
- That our purpose be His Purpose
- That our plan be His Plan
- That our will be His Will
- That we flee from what He Flees

All this my friends, is found in God's Most Holy Word

We must be intentional in mirroring, replicating, and copying the example of Jesus' Life:

- This is Glorifying God, taking on His Character, then fleshing it out in this fallen world.
- When we do this, we do this with the motive of LOVE, drawing people to Jesus Christ for Salvation.
- We are co-labouring with Jesus winning souls for Our Father, in love and patience. Amen

That all may be reconciled and none should perish

(1 John 4:16-19)
God is love. Whoever lives in love lives in God, and God in him. 17 In this way, love is made complete among us so that we will have confidence on the day of judgment, because in this world we are like him. There is no fear in love. But perfect love drives out fear, because fear has to do with punishment. The one who fears is not made perfect in love.19 We love because he first loved us.

``***We love because he first loved us***``.

In all, we are frustrated with our personal Christian spiritual growth.

Why?

Because we desire to love and obey God. We have fallen into a pit, a trap, a snare, even a net, stopping us from giving glory to the Lord. Next we are going to look at the elements that stop us from adopting our dear Father's Character.

All of us are or have been entrapped in habitual sin, where the devil is accusing us to the Father daily, and when he does accuse us, he accuses us of real guilt!

- This is where we are practicing sin
- The allure of sin has trapped us in bondage

- Once we are aware of the Truth of the Father's Love for us, we are helpless to escape the Truth
- We are without excuse

We love because he first loved us.

Once the Truth of God`s Love is exposed to the heart, the lie of the devil is exposed plainly as well.

- This is the time to act, fight, reject, deny, and trade the lie for the Truth of God`s Love
- We need to adopt the Truth of God`s Love, and embrace the Truth of God`s Love, and love the Truth of God`s Love
- We need to hate the lie, abhor the lie, and finally, mortify the lie

Our Father sees us as a people who have taken refuge in His Son and that we are worthy of His Love. Know this brothers and sisters we are Loved, and we have always been Loved.

With this knowledge we need to be restored by lifting up the Truth of God`s Love, with gladness and cheer and with celebrating daily, weekly, monthly, and yearly. We should be always looking to the Love of the Father for our refuge and do all things without grumbling, especially in light of what Jesus Our Lord has done on our behalf.

We need the Saviour; we need to be free from the lie once and for all and in this chapter we are going to look at the steps we need to take to come into alignment with the Will of the Father for our lives, our sanctification, holiness and consecration.

We must keep fighting the good fight of believing the Truth of God's Word because if we do, we will be rewarded

- By having more of heaven now!
- More of the peace that surpasses understanding now!

- We can be more like Him now!
- We can adopt His Likeness, Image, Nature, and Character more now!

Jesus is just waiting for us to come out of the darkness and stop harboring our sins and step into the marvelous light of confessing our sins which give birth to repenting and in the end, Eternal Life.

- He will forgive us
- He will give us the strength and courage to turn from our sins today
- He will even aid us, in smashing our idols and destroying our vices
- He will chase us from our sexual immorality
- He will instruct us to flee, if need be
- He will cleanse us from all unrighteousness.

1 John 1:8
8 If we claim to be without sin, we deceive ourselves and the truth is not in us.

Yes! We are sinners made saints, the Lord calls us just before we are made just, and He calls us righteous before we are made righteous.

- In Christ, we are holy, just, and righteous.
- We are not inherently holy, just, and righteous in and of ourselves that no one may boast of it
- But by the imputation of Jesus' Righteousness, we are declared Justified in God's eyes
- We are forgiven

No one is without sin because it only takes one sin to be a sinner.

- God has set forward His Mandate for us to be a holy and righteous people, a peculiar people, set apart for His Glory.

- But know this, we all fail this Mandate.
- So to declare before man and to declare before God that we are without sin ***we deceive ourselves and the truth is not in us.***

1 John 1:9 9 If we confess our sins, he is faithful and just and will forgive us our sins and purify us from all unrighteousness.

- In this, it is He Who Justifies us, and it is He Who Sanctifies us
- He will cleanse us from all unrighteousness
- He will Glorify us.

For this purification happens, not so that we sin more or less, but that we confess our sin, we name our sin, and we repent of our sin that we already have.

- The sin we already have becomes more evident to us and the severity is exposed to us in the Truth of God's Word alone
- By keeping with repentance we will bear the fruits that Jesus Desires us to bear, that none should perish, but that all would come to repentance and find Mercy in the Lord and thus find hope
- The Truth of God's Word is the only source that can binds the conscience, and enables us to bear the fruit
- The end result is that we turn from the lie and adopt the Truth without grumbling
- We gladly and cheerfully embrace the Truth
- This can only happen through the Father causing us to walk in His Precepts and Status and to be careful to obey His Law by Faith

We know that most learn from time, trial, and error, but we learn from the Fatherhood of God

Those He loves, He disciplines. He is the Chief Shepherd and His Rod and His Staff they ought to comfort us as abiding disciples and students of His Word.

- This is where He ***purifies us from all unrighteousness.***

1 John 1:10 [10]If we claim we have not sinned, we make him out to be a liar and his word has no place in our lives.

- Yes! If we say we have not sinned, we call God a liar who declares us to be Lawbreakers
- We are all accountable to God Our Father, not one sin will go unpunished
- The Gospel has no place in our lives if we do not repent and confess our sin, especially in light of what Jesus has done on our behalf

But if we confess our sin, He is ***faithful and just and will forgive us our sins and purify us from all unrighteousness***

- So all mankind's sin will either be forgiven or judged justly
- Those that do repent have Faith in Christ, they will be forgiven and cleansed as white as snow
- When we behold His Glory we shall be like Him, for we shall see Him as He is
- Know this, in the end we will be purged of all Indwelling Sin and the practice thereof
- One day we will be holy and separate from the presence of sin
- He will cleanse us from all unrighteousness
- This can only happen through the One who is qualified to be the Saviour, by Him, who Sanctified Himself.

Jesus is His name!

(Rom 3:23-24) for all have sinned and fall short of the glory of God

Our words, action, thoughts, and the motives of our hearts have to be perfectly and continually righteous without one fracture of error to bring Glory to the Father.

- We have ***all have sinned and fall short of the glory of God***. Not one of us is righteous, not one!!
- We do not sin "just because" we sin brothers and sisters, but no! Friends we sin because we are sinners to the very core, each and every one of us
- This is all we have ever known

We have no perfect inherent righteousness in and of ourselves, nor can we manufacture it.

But we do have:

The Great Exchange

- Our sins for Christ's Righteousness
- Our sins for His Grace
- Our sin for His Charity

We Have:

Jesus Christ's Inherent Righteousness imputed to us.
Jesus Christ's Inherent Teachings imparted to us.
Jesus Christ's Inherent Example shown to us.

In keeping with repentance we will bear such lush fruits as:

- The Father's Image as we honorable represent His Holy Name
- The Father's Likeness as we honorable represent His Holy Name
- The Father's Nature as we honorable represent His Holy Name
- and finally, The Father's Character as we honorable represent His Holy Name

(Isa 64:6)
All of us have become like one who is unclean,
and all our righteous acts are like filthy rags; we all shrivel up like a leaf and like the wind our sins sweep us away

The Characteristics and Identity of a Christian

We Shall Be Like Him

Chapter 12

The Characteristics and Identity of a Christian

We Shall Be Like Him

Chapter 12

(1 John 3:2)[2] ***Dear friends, now we are children of God, and what we will be has not yet been made known. But we know that when Christ appears, we shall be like him, for we shall see him as he is.***

This is the Truth of God's Word, with all its clarity ***what we will be has not yet been made known.*** Meaning this is God's Hidden Will for us. We do not know what we will be yet, but at this time, we know that ***now we are children of God,*** this is the Truth of God's Word ***now we are children of God and what we will be has not yet been made known***.

Next the text expounds what will take place ***but we know that when Christ appears, we shall be like him. when he appears we shall be like him.***

Why?

for we shall see him as he is. We will behold His Glory and in His Glory, the Father will glorify the workmanship of His hands.

(John 15:5)[5] ***"I am the vine; you are the branches. <u>If you remain in me and I in you, you will bear much fruit; apart from me you can do nothing.</u>***

So, apart from Christ we can do nothing, but this does not mean we do nothing!

- We as professing Christians, must see the necessity of cooperating with the person of the Holy Spirit, in the work of our personal sanctification, (our being cleansed from all unrighteousness)
- We will be blameless children, set apart for the Father's Glory
- There are no chains of bondage, no grip of debauchery and no hold on sin, that His Love can't break

Believe that you are freed from the triad, and save to God and to righteousness

(Rom 6:6-8)
6 For we know that our old self was crucified with him so that the body of sin might be done away with that we should no longer be slaves to sin— 7 because anyone who has died has been freed from sin.
8 Now if we died with Christ, we believe that we will also live with him.

Have Faith in God that you have been delivered from the domain of darkness and have been transferred into the Kingdom of Light.

To be made like Jesus.

- We are a work in progress and we must never underestimate the sufficiency of God's Grace in our lives.

He is working in us and through us for:

- His good Pleasure,
- His good Will,
- His good Plan,
- His good Purposes.

Believe that the Lord's ***grace is sufficient for you***

(2 Cur 12:7-10)
7 To keep me from becoming conceited because of these surpassingly great revelations, there was given me a thorn in my flesh, a messenger of Satan, to torment me. 8 Three times I pleaded with the Lord to take it away from me. 9 But he said to me, "My grace is sufficient for you, for my power is made perfect in weakness." Therefore, I will boast all the more gladly about my weaknesses, so that Christ's power may rest on me. 10 That is why, for Christ's sake, I delight in weaknesses, in insults, in hardships, in persecutions, in difficulties. For when I am weak, then I am strong.

Believe and have Faith that your name is written in the Book of Life and you belong to the Lamb that was Slain for our sins as was decided before the creation of the world!

Now do good works in the name of Jesus!

- Always give Glory to God
- Always act in loving kindness
- Always do justice
- Always walk humbly with God
- Always be quick to do mercy to all with a cheerful heart and a glad Spirit
- Always labour in drawing people to God Our Father
- Above all Always love one another as God Commanded

Because this is the Work of Christ: **reconciling creation back to their creator**.

How?

- Jesus gave us the means to ***become the righteousness of God.***

This is the good news distilled:

- He imputes His Righteousness to us and we imputed our sin to Him

- He took them away in this Great Exchange
- He reconciled us back to the Father
- We, who believe, receive His Gift by the Instrumental Cause of Faith
- Then we labour in drawing people to God to receive the Gifted Merit of His Son Jesus Christ
- We are justified because of an alien righteousness, that is not our own, a perfect and continuous righteousness, outside of ourselves

Therefore, we receive the wage Jesus earned, and He Expiates our sins and thus made Propitiation by His Blood. The Fruits of His Labour are given to us as a Gift, by the Father's Grace and Mercy and Compassion!

In this way, nothing we have done or will do is sufficient in satisfying God's Wrath. Only the sinless Son of God and His Blood Offering on our behalf as a substitution payment for our sins and crimes. Therefore, because of His Atonement, He perfectly satisfying the righteous hostility that God had towards our sin.

- Jesus the Christ, died to make a once and for all Atonement for our sin, and to appease God's Wrath, which He had against our sins and treasonous crimes
- However, that is not the end of the story, because He did not only die for our sins, He lived for our righteousness
- He lived to reconcile us back to God
- The only way we can come into the presence of God is to be sinless

This is our reconciliation: Jesus lived a perfectly and continually sinless life to offer the Fruits of His Labour to us all as a Love Gift.

- The Father gave His Son as a Love Gift; this is why we give ourselves as a Love Gift to God
- God gave us His Son as a Love Gift

- The Holy Spirit loves us and continually reveals the depths of God's Love for us who have Faith and Believe
- Thus, as the Son Loves the Father the Father Loves the Son and has given Him the Full Measure of His Spirit and has given all things into His Hand
- The Spirit reveals the Son's Authority and in His Reign as He sits at the Right Hand of the Father on High.

(2Cor 5:18-21)
[18] All this is from God, who reconciled us to himself through Christ and gave us the ministry of reconciliation: [19] that God was reconciling the world to himself in Christ, not counting men's sins against them. And he has committed to us the message of reconciliation. [20] We are therefore Christ's ambassadors, as though God were making his appeal through us. We implore you on Christ's behalf: Be reconciled to God. [21] God made him who had no sin to be sin for us, so that in him we might become the righteousness of God.

Our Father raised His Son from the grave, resurrecting Him in the Body. This is what He wants to do for us in Christ, before all the living and the dead; for His Glory.

(2 Cor 5:14-15[14] For Christ's love compels us, because we are convinced that one died for all, and therefore all died. [15] And he died for all, that those who live should no longer live for themselves but for him who died for them and was raised again.

The Characteristics and Identity of a Christian

We Will Have Hard Times

Chapter 13

The Characteristics and Identity of a Christian

We Will Have Hard Times

Chapter 13

We all have obstacles on the narrow path to conform to Jesus the Son of the Living God.

Believe me, we have:

- The pit
- The snare
- The trap
- And the net

The worst thing is we're on the defensive side in an of ourselves, but we have Faith & Hope in Christ.

Brothers and sisters, we are Now In Christ, and He is on the offensive side.

Why?

Because He is the Stronger Man, ***(Luke 11:21-22)21 "When a strong man, fully armed, guards his own house, his possessions are safe. 22 But when someone stronger attacks and overpowers him, he takes away the armor in which the man trusted and divides up the spoils.*** Jesus is the Stronger Man, He is fully capable to attack and overpower the devil. Jesus takes away the Triad's armor and destroys his stronghold in our thinking, which is the lie in which we sadly trusted.

We are the Children of God if we believe the Truth of God and our Faith is in Him, the strongest whom raised Jesus from the dead. Therefore, He spoke creation into existence.

He created:

- The darkness and the light
- Calamity and wellbeing
- Mercy and judgment
- Death and life

So if God is for us who can be against us?

We are on the offensive side alongside Jesus, if we are within His Will; our Sanctification. This is and will always be His Will for us as Christians: our holiness, our consecration, our righteousness, and our godliness is His Will for us Christians to attain and walk in.

Take heart, take courage, be reconciled to God Our Father. Therefore, with man, all things are impossible, but with God all things are possible.

It is possible to:

- Stand for the Truth of His Word
- Live for the Truth of His Word
- Fight for the Truth His Word
- If need be we die for the Truth of His Word

(John 17:14-19) I have given them your word and the world has hated them, for they are not of the world any more than I am of the world. 15 My prayer is not that you take them out of the world but that you protect them from the evil one. 16 They are not of the world, even as I am not of it. 17 Sanctify them by the truth; your word is truth. 18 As you sent me into the world, I have sent them into the world. 19 For them I sanctify myself, that they too may be truly sanctified.

As believers, would we live, fight or even die for the Truth of God's Word?

We need to know that God's Word is Infallible, Immutable, Impeccable and Inerrant, so may it never be that we who are associating ourselves with God, associate ourselves with the devil. The world is living in half truths, but we ought to be the first to walk and abide in the Objective Truth, and lead others to do the same.

Are we right now:

- Living
- Fighting
- And willing to die for the devil?

The devil is the fallen spirit that is working in the sons of disobedience.

We must not:

- Live
- Fight
- Or die for the world

The world is the fallen nature around us and in us on this earth.

We must not:

- Live
- Fight
- Or die for the flesh

The flesh is our individual fallen sinful nature we all have.

We do not live, fight or die for the lies of the triad. But no! We live, fight, and die for the Truth of the Triune God, we serve and worship.

Why?

Because we are not on the defensive side anymore, but on the offensive side against:

- Sin
- Satan
- Death

Just as Jesus is, we are fighting the Good Fight Alongside Him, our Sovereign King.

We have to stop and look at ourselves. Are we building up the Kingdom or tearing it down?

- Pride
- Ego
- Arrogance

Tear the Kingdom apart!

Humility, love, and patience always build up His Kingdom, and by building His Kingdom we exalt His Kingship, for Jesus is the King.

All of creation is His! He has Sovereign Authority, Dominion and Power over everything. He is Sovereign over Life, Death, Judgment and all Matter.

- As Christians, we fight to crucify the flesh, this is our character. Therefore, if you are not fighting the war against sin or rejecting conformity to the world, the devil, and the flesh right now in your life, you're not a Christian. Is this too crass to say friends?

You may ask why?

Dear brothers and sisters, because that is the Christian Character. Our Lord Demands Victory over sin, Satan, the world, and our flesh, even further, death. Our lives ought to be a reflection of Christ's Life: Glory to Glory! Victory to Victory!

1Timothy 6:12) [12] ***Fight the good fight of faith, lay hold on eternal life, to which you were also called and have confessed the good confession in the presence of many witnesses.***

- We will suffer with Christ, but may it never be for sin's sake, let it be instead for righteousness' sake. Then and only then, will we share in His Suffering.

Why?

Because Jesus, suffered for righteousness sake, He died for our sin, yes! But rose for our righteousness. He alone freely gives the Gift of Eternal Life in the Paradise of God. Thus, by God's Grace we have been saved through Faith. This Gift must abide in the Christian's mind forever. Thus, through Faith we receive this Gift, the very sign and seal of our redemption: The very Spirit of Truth.

Therefore, know this and believe this, that we are weak but Jesus is Strong. Know also, that He has over come the world, the devil, and the flesh and He has received victory and glory, for conquering the domain of darkness and setting the captives free. Therefore, He offers us the same victory and glory through Faith in Him and His power to Save the Soul from the enemy.

We have Hope!

(1 John 5:1-4) 5 Whoever believes that Jesus is the Christ is born of God, and everyone who loves Him who begot also loves him who is begotten of Him. [2] ***By this we know that we love the children of God, when we love God and keep His commandments.*** [3] ***For this is the love of God, that we keep His commandments. And His commandments are not burdensome.*** [4] ***For whatever is born of God overcomes the***

world. And this is the victory that has overcome the world—our faith.

What is the nature of the pit, the snare, the trap, and the net?

The nature of the pit, the snare, the trap, and the net, is that as we walk on the path to life we quickly find out that fallen humanity is all around us and has laid a pit before us to fall into. Then the devil sets a snare for our flesh, and the flesh has invited in the spirit that is now working in the sons of disobedience.

But!

- ***(Psalm 9:9[9] The LORD also will be a refuge for the oppressed, A refuge in times of trouble.***
- ***(Psalm 18:2)[2] The LORD is my rock and my fortress and my deliverer; My God, my strength, in whom I will trust; My shield and the horn of my salvation, my stronghold.***
- ***(Nahum 1:7)[7] The LORD is good, a stronghold in the day of trouble; And He knows those who trust in Him.***

Every day brothers and sisters, we are at war alongside Jesus.

Jesus, is our rear guard as well as our front guard He is our Refuge. We all must be on guard and alert, not merely prepared but be vigilant in and of our selves, walking in preparedness, and being ready for war with military precision. Read the Word of God!

1 Peter 1:13-16
13 Therefore, prepare your minds for action; be self-controlled; set your hope fully on the grace to be given you when Jesus Christ is revealed. 14 As obedient children, do not conform to the evil desires you had when you lived in ignorance. 15 But just as he who called you is holy, so be holy in all you do; 16 for it is written: "Be holy, because I am holy."

There is a battle going on in everyone's life. The war is generated by fighting for the Truth of God's Word. This battle is against the flesh, the world, and the devil who is the triad, we must not trade the Truth of God's Word for the lie, period!

Why?

Because if we do, we then will begin to believe the lie. This would be total depravity. This is where the Good Lord found us all:

- Believing the lie
- We are all like sheep being led astray by the lie

However, if we walk in humility before God, we will always choose the Truth and submit to the Truth. The only alternative to this is to disobey the Truth of God's Word and puff up with pride and submit to no one.

(Rom 1:24-25)
24 Therefore God gave them over in the sinful desires of their hearts to sexual impurity for the degrading of their bodies with one another. 25 They exchanged the truth of God for a lie, and worshiped and served created things rather than the Creator — who is forever praised. Amen.

We know the abundance of grace with which we have received, there is no end.

We will be enabled by the power of the Holy Ghost to turn from sin. So know that this fight we are engaging in can only be authored through the Enabling Power of the Holy Spirit, whom energizes us and is convicting us with the Truth of God's Word, by cutting us who believe, straight through the heart.

- We are all very tired of being hearers only of God's Word, but we desire to be true listeners and doers of God's Word

- The Christian ought to desire and acclaim to draw people to Jesus, in this we will succeed, because this is within God's Will
- Not only to be hearers of God's Word, but to actually listen and be doers of His Word, living by the Truth of God's Word. The power of His Spirit exposes us to the Truth of His Word and His Word can only reveal the depths of Himself and His Love to us who believe.

Therefore, we are being hemmed in on all sides by the devil, and the world, for they are catering to the desires of our flesh, moment to moment. Sadly, friends, this is all we have ever known since childhood. We are sinners in our mother's womb because Adam's sin fell upon us. Our sinful nature is why we need to walk in the Spirit, that we will not gratify the desires of the flesh. The Spirit searches the depths, cares, and desires of God, revealing His Way to us so that we may adopt His Way gladly and cheerfully from the heart.

Christians, we must conform to Jesus Christ. Therefore, our fallen sinful nature is all around us, but sadly, this sinful nature is in us as well.

This is why we need to seek, ask, and knock, for the:

- Knowledge of how to submit to the Desires of the Father
- Knowledge of how to please the Father
- Knowledge of how to honorably love the Father

Why?

Because, we are sinners to the core. Better said, "We do not sin because we sin" but no! "We sin because we are sinners, to the core, at the very heart we are sinners." We need the heart to change to have life in us, so pray for the heart to change.

(2 Peter 1:3-9)*[3] *as His divine power has given to us all things that pertain to life and godliness, through the knowledge of Him who called us by glory and virtue,* [4] *by which have been

given to us exceedingly great and precious promises, that through these you may be partakers of the divine nature, having escaped the corruption that is in the world through lust.[5] But also for this very reason, giving all diligence, add to your faith virtue, to virtue knowledge, [6] to knowledge self-control, to self-control perseverance, to perseverance godliness, [7] to godliness brotherly kindness, and to brotherly kindness love. [8] For if these things are yours and abound, you will be neither barren nor unfruitful in the knowledge of our Lord Jesus Christ. [9] For he who lacks these things is short sighted, even to blindness, and has forgotten that he was cleansed from his old sins.

We are all desiring a mighty change in our hearts as transformed Christians, we want to please the Father and if we could, we would be perfectly holy and righteous. This is our Christian desire to not be bothered with death, sin, and debauchery, these are like a big rock in our shoe. We want to be blameless, pure, and righteous.

Therefore, when the Lord come to gather His People, they desire to be received. In order for us to choose the Truth over the lie, we must be well aware of the allure of the lie and we need to grasp that the Lord will always offer a way of escape to anyone willing to surrender their lives over to Him. The one who has All Authority to crush the head of the serpent, is Jesus and no other.

Lastly, I pray the lie will never oppress the Christian. Believing the lie and practicing it, there is no happy ending for such a person. We have the Truth of God's Word written on our hearts, but know this; you have been delivered from the domain of darkness and have been transferred into the Kingdom of Light (death to life), from the lie to the Truth, and from bondage to freedom. Amen

1 Cor 10:11-13

11 These things happened to them as examples and were written down as warnings for us, on whom the fulfillment of

the ages has come. 12 So, if you think you are standing firm, be careful that you don't fall! 13 No temptation has seized you except what is common to man. And God is faithful; he will not let you be tempted beyond what you can bear. But when you are tempted, he will also provide a way out so that you can stand up under it.

The Truth shall set you Free
And if He sets you free
You will be free indeed

The Characteristics and Identity of a Christian

Testimony

Chapter 14

The Characteristics and Identity of a Christian

Testimony

Chapter 14

Dear friends, this is my testimony.

- I was self-seeking and turned inward, not caring for others or seeking God but satisfying inward desires of all kinds of evil, and the passions of my flesh consumed me like a fox in a rattlesnake den.
- I had traded the Truth for a lie; I had worshiped the creature comforts rather than the creator. I loved them, and never thought that I would one day stand before God and give an account of my life.
- I was in the dark, dead in my sin, and I was going to die in my sin and be sent to hell for my sin. I was hell bound.
- And my flesh loved it because the world and the devil gave me everything I desired.
- But the worst thing is that this is all I ever new, radical depravity.

  - Crashing waves of regret and shame and guilt. God's Wrath was upon me: the unrighteous, the sinner, the law breaker, the unjust, the wicked, the evil, like a horse running head long into battle, was I who ran to sin; I craved it; I was totally lost and helpless to my vices and spiritually dead to my first love, Jesus Christ.
  - "I was deaf to His Call to Life and I was dead in my trespasses and sins."

- I was living in a hotel: homeless, friendless, motherless, fatherless, penniless, Godless, unredeemed, unsaved, helpless, heavily addicted, and lost. I was blind to the spiritual realm and deaf to the Voice of God that I once heard. I was dead in my sins, without hope, and spiritually separated from the commonwealth of God and the richness of His Kingdom. I was eating at a soup kitchen and just eking out my existence through life.
- "But" is the best word I know. But!! God being rich in mercy revealed Himself to me one night. I was in a hotel and I opened the night table drawer and picked up a Bible and God was calling me. I stopped everything and opened it. God spoke to me right away in book of Psalms; He pierced my heart with light and I was forever changed. I began bawling and repenting and begging for His promises to take root in my life. I was helplessly and humbly asking for forgiveness of my sin. I was broken before God and asked Jesus to forgive me and make everything right with His Father, for me.
- The key thing we soon forget is that our Father is Holy
- Right there, I saw God's holiness and my ungodliness.

I saw that Christ is the great Savior and I am a great sinner.
As I read more of God`s Word, I was captivated.
I gave my heart to Jesus, I read His Gospel, and I said to Him, "My heart is yours; do with me as you wish."
He had given me a new heart.
He had given life to my dead spirit.
I once sought out the things Christ hated.
But through His rich mercy, I now love the things Christ loves, such as His people, His church, and bringing glory to His Glories Father Rejoice!
You have given me what I need: **The Holy Spirit! Rejoice!**
I worship you with all my heart, I praise you with my tongue, and I boast about you among the people.
I thank you and praise you because you are awesome and praise worthy. Rejoice!

- I have been pursuing Christ, my Savior, and God, rejoice! In the Lord the giver of life. We are all birthed into the Kingdom, but by God rejoice! In the compassion and mercy of God by giving us his Son to die on our behalf. Rejoice! There is nothing I can do but pray for you and ask God to reveal Himself to you so that you will be heaven bound. Rejoice!
- So grab the Holy Bible, open it, and see, hear, and taste that the Lord is good and sweet to the soul.

Brothers and sisters, we all have a story to tell, but the best thing is that the Lord was and is ALWAYS there. We are all saved by God, for it has always been God who took the initiative in all our lives to save us from the condemnation of His Law. Have you come into a saving relationship with Jesus? If not, I will pray for you. Remember, our God loved us first. The Scriptures say that God, out of His Great Love, chose us before the creation of the world. He actually chose us and predestined us to obtain salvation in His Son before we were formed in our mother`s womb.

- I stand here not in arrogance of the assured gift received, but in the humility of one who repents and confesses his sins to his creator: "Please, Father, forgive us our sins; have mercy on me a sinner."
- All our hope is in the refuge of Christ, The Father's Son, and His righteous life imputed to our bankrupt accounts not cancelling the debt of our sin but paying for it in full. Father, thank you! for giving us life when we had no life; "Awesome is your name. Amen."
- **Just to finish!**

Brothers, sisters, and neighbors.
I was asked to give my testimony today. I will finish with my present way of life.

I speak to the Lord in the morning;
during the day I walk with Him.
I confide in the Lord in times of need.
The Lord is my Father; He loves me and wants to see me
succeed in holiness, righteousness, and godliness.
The Lord has a pure heart.
Through Him all things can be done.
At night I am alone; the day has passed, and the Lord
comforts me; and I am safe.
When I lay my head down, I speak to God; He hears my case,
my worries, my thoughts, and my desires.
I am not alone; I am in the presence of the Most High.
I am comfortable in His presence;
I yearn to make Him proud.
And I love the Lord.
Jesus is His name. Amen.
I praise the Lord as I open my eyes; I greet Him.
The day is full of things unknown, but
I am secure in the Lord and willing to face the day in
faith.
When turbulent water arises, the Lord's Prayer is in my
heart and on my tongue.
I praise God and look back on what He has done: my life
has been saved,
spared from the cords of death, addiction, and the final judgment
of my soul. Christ has paid my ransom to the Father and has
redeemed me from hell—
"it is finished."
He forgives me in his great mercies and I love Him.
He is with me always until the end.
My charter has been renewed.
The Lord has given me back my dignity.
My identity has been redeemed.
The Lord has given me peace on all sides;
the image of Christ is being restored
in me through the refining fires of sanctification—
all praise and worship I give to God.

His heart is pure and good.
His Word is sweet to my soul.
I read it every day, and I love to meditate on it and fill my heart with its Truth and Grace, and my spirit is at peace with God.
He leads me down a straight path so that my heart might be right with Him always and forever as I await the coming of His Son, who will rule and reign and judge this world.
He is full of mercy.
So repent to the Lord and follow the commandments.
And fear God for He does not wish to see us perish.
But rest on His refuge, not our own self-reliance; rest on His strength, not our own might. For apart from Him, we can do nothing.

The Characteristics and Identity of a Christian

We Have Strength and Hope Against the Enemy

Chapter 15

The Characteristics and Identity of a Christian

We Have Strength and Hope Against the Enemy

Chapter 15

We have strength and hope against the enemy

The God we worship is not like us; in one big way he is very, very different. God is self-existent. "Aseity" is the word that we use to define this. For the Aseity of God refers to Him having His Existence in and of Himself. This is what defines the Supremacy of the Supreme Being; God is the Supreme Being. We are human beings, His angels are Angelic Beings, and God is the Supreme Being. He is fully Sovereign, meaning He has Supreme Authority over all creation. He is highest in rank and authority; He is the paramount, Exalted Chief. God is not a creature. Our lives are fragile, but God cannot die. There is nothing that is out of His power or out of His reach; He is not dependent upon anything or anyone for His being. He has the very power of being in and of Himself, which is the very thing we do not have. He can create all things by the power of His Command, or as we say, His Word. No one made God; He is Eternal from the beginning to the end; He is Infinite and He has the power to sustain His creation, everywhere and at all times. He is transcendent over His creation, in the heavens and on earth, meaning He is governing His creation from above, independent over all the universe and time. But our God is Imminent as well; He is near and always at hand. He is Omnipresent, in all places and at all times. What I am trying to say is that the war we fight is fickle and minute compared to the power of the Omnipotent God we serve.

In Scripture, the Power of God is the cross; this is our refuge from the flesh and the condemnation of the law that says that we are powerless and that the law has all the power in our lives to send us to hell. The world wants us to rely on the law to save us but it always cuts us to the knees. The weakness of our flesh in this fallen world is the devil's stronghold, not God's Holy Law. However, our inability to carry out the demands of the law; the devil perverts, defiles, and exploits our fleshly passions that reduce us to slaves of darkness and the failure of the law, leaving us condemned under the law. We need a Saviour truly and true genuine Saviour.

The defenses of secular people are down, and they do not have the stronger man, our victorious Lord, to protect them as we do because they have no Authoritative Truth and do not know the redeeming grace of the cross. But we have this Truth—we have God's Grace—and we have the name of Jesus on our lips, and we have consummated Him in our heart. We have His Spirit in us, and we cling to the cross, because the cross is the Power of God. The law cuts us all to the knees and no one can stand, but the cross brings us all to level ground, where we willingly kneel down to our Savior and surrender our lives to His Saving Arms. Christians, we must choose the Lord, not the law, to save us because the law is there to direct us to Jesus that he alone can save us from condemnation of the law, which each of us fails perpetually. Jesus is our Savour.

Angel Army

We will have victory, yes, we will be delivered into the Kingdom and into the presence of our wonderful amazing Father, who is so gracious, kind, and loving that His Son will usher us in, and all the angels will be filled with joy for the battle is won. You know and I know, brothers and sisters, that there is no ignorance among you and that the battle is here, my brothers and sisters, right before your very eyes—just rub your eyes so that you can see the enemy all around you. And the army of angels like Joel 2: 7-11 ***warriors they charge; like soldiers they scale the wall. They march each on his way; they do not swerve from their path. They do not jostle one another; each march's in his path; they burst through the weapons and are not halted. They leap upon that walls, they climb up into the houses, and they enter through the window like a thief. The earth quakes before them; the heavens tremble. The stars withdraw their shining. The Lord utters his voice before his army, for his camp is exceedingly great; he who executes his word is powerful. For the day of the Lord is great and very awesome; who can endure it?***

Pray always that the Holy Spirit convicts you of your sin so that you do not deceive yourself and think that you have no sin in your life. Pray to see the powers that are veiled working in this redemptive realm, which you have been qualified to partake in. You are in the realm of the eternal, and the angelic beings are there always in this realm; faith will reveal all of this to you. Therefore, you can discern the direction that leads to heaven so that you may be forever heaven bound.

Fight, have victory, and win by abiding in the Lord so that He will always abide in you. Amen. God predestined us beforehand, before the world was formed and before we were formed in our mother's womb so that we would come to the fullness of holiness and be sanctified, which means to be made holy. His foreknowledge is that we are His Elect, His Chosen, and we, as believers, are preordained to be holy and consecrated for service to the King and to the Kingdom: "Thy will be done on earth as it is in heaven." Amen.

Ephesians 1:4 New International Version (NIV)

[4] ***For he chose us in him before the creation of the world to be holy and blameless in his sight. In love***

Victory in love

Victory over the devil and death once and for all, this is the promise we trust in. We, as Christians, are God's People, set apart for holiness, and our victory is in God's Son's name, Jesus Christ, the name above all names. He is the Truth that sets us free. The consummation of Christ's Nature in our hearts is the Gospel's promise. Therefore, truly all our ability is from the Holy Spirit's dependence and His Energizing Power to sustain and bring forth growth in all things. It is only by this will that we are enabled to have the desire to please God and bring Him joy. It is only in this mind-set that we can sustain any level of obedience that is flowing from the heart, be willing to be faithful to God, and submit and surrender to Christ's Lordship in this life. Our obedience is of the will, yes! But our obedience is enabled by the Holy Spirit because the will of man is in bondage—no one can come to God unless he or she is enabled to respond to the Gospel by the life-giving enabler, the Holy Spirit of God Himself.

Scripture says that our will is in bondage to sin, but actually, it is in slavery to Satan, the father of all sin and lies. However, Christ is the Mighty Savior who frees us from that bondage and liberates us and delivers us. For the Truth sets us free, and our obedience needs to be a sacrificial offering to God out of a grateful heart; we are His slaves now, bought and paid for with the Blood of Christ. Do not forget that we have been purchased.

Furthermore, the Father has taken ownership of us. We were not a redeemed people and chosen for the glory of man, this world, the devil, or the demons, but for God in His great love and to His Awesome Glory, which is solely due His Name. We are His and nothing can separate us from Him and His Love. He has fought for our salvation, and our identity is in Him alone. So, be satisfied, Christian, and be grateful and live in love! Live in love! As a living sacrifice, offer your life as a fragrant offering, peaceable, righteous, and just. Therefore, always walk humbly with your God and pray to the Holy Spirit that your passion be filled and your zeal for the Gospel be opened up to this fallen world; pray for a revival of our loved ones; we are not forgotten, but we Christians rest on God's Unfailing Love.

This is the first step to sanctification, desiring to do the purpose and will and plan of God in His Saving Enterprise. Believers must be energized, motivated, submissive, and dependent on the power of the Holy Spirit if we, individually and as a collective body, are to be successful in carrying out the duty that is set before us. A life of piety leads to reverence and will always uphold the integrity of Christ Jesus, our Lord and Savior. So a pious life that is reverent to Holy God will make one meek, not a defender of self, but a defender of God. One who is reverent will always lift God up and protect His integrity as well as Christ's Church.

Our hearts are calling out to our creator as we attempt to embrace the light and come out of the dark. All Christians around the world are going through this, so you need never feel alone; we are all fighting this battle every day. Therefore, repentance is a Christian's life, obedience is a Christian's desire, and God's Favor is everything—nothing is to be more treasured than God's joy in our life. Those who have heard the call from Christ, had their affections drawn to Him, and been convicted by the Truth need to follow the Good Shepherd who loves, feeds, and tends the flock for eternity. You can be like Him, and once you are brought into conformity, you will desire and love the things He desires and loves and hate the things He hates. You will be holy as He is holy and sacred as He is sacred and consecrated as He is consecrated; you will be ready to do good works and service in the Kingdom to the Glory of God. This is the reason Christ brought the Gospel to deliver us from slavery to and oppression by the sin of this corrupted, fallen world.

Christ has paid the ransom to the Father for our sins so that He might appease God's righteous judgment of us. Christ Jesus, our Lord, loved us so much He took our punishment for us and purchased us by His blood. He said, "It is finished." We are

His people, and He puts us forward with love—with the great command of love. We are to have hearts that have surpassing gratitude because we love our neighbor, we love God, we love His Law, and we love pleasing Our Father. Christ is our treasure; He is the "door," the only access to the Father and into heaven is through Him. We can see He loves us; we just have to have faith that we will be sanctified and with Him soon. We must fight this battle with a love that will be victorious over sin. Be conscious of God and do not mock Him because He is always present, brother and sisters; He resides in our lives and in our hearts. Do not grieve the Spirit of God that is in us, but love Him and demonstrate His love to all.

No one will ever be able to thank God unless he or she has succeeded in pleasing the Father, our God. Because of our sinful self-pleasing and self-destructive nature, we know this is our weakness and fear. But love casts out weakness and fear, and we should be the most courageous, enduring, and mighty people on this plant because we have the incarnation of God's Spirit in us, with us, and through us. Do not hinder the Spirit of love, but promote Him always because humility and love are the mark of a Christian! We are to be self-sacrificing in pleasing God, meaning our time, talents, and treasures should align with or conform to God's will and promote the promise of redemption in an honorable manner, never looking for a reward.

We are the servant and the Lord God is the Master; we serve Him first, then others, and then ourselves last. We are here for only a little while, brothers and sisters, so we must humble ourselves and serve in love in order to be exalted. Those who exalt themselves will be brought low in the Kingdom; and those who have not thanked God with all their heart and without misgiving or reservation do not know what joy is. Because true joy comes from pleasing God, and true thanksgiving comes when God enables us to please Him.

Therefore, the supernatural power of the Holy Spirit quickens, renews, regenerates, and transforms our being to perfectly sustain a grateful, joyous, righteous, honorable, holy, and pure heart toward our God. Those who have pure hearts will see God. This is victory, brothers and sisters. Although we are weak in an instant and may stumble, we have the Lord to forgive our sin if we repent. We will not fall headlong and dash our faces on the ground because the Lord sustains us, and His love holds us up, and His Word rebukes, corrects, instructs, and trains us in rightness and godliness. Never turn your back on the work of sharing the good news, but "Repent for the Kingdom of God is at hand."

Do not become cold or lukewarm; fervent zeal and passion are hot—this is the love we need, fellow believers, a love that is hot and intentional, a love that is on fire and boiling over. The God we worship is like a burning bush that never goes out. He is never quenched, so we must never quench the spirit of love!

Always be hungry for the Word, like one who starves in a famine. Seek, ask, knock, and run after the Truth in Scripture: seek always the Truth, not phrases that sound good to the ear—love the Truth! My prayer to those who are reading this right now is to love your enemies, pray for them day and night so that they will come out of the dark and into the light; forgive them because we only have a short time left here. All who do not believe will perish in the flames, so love them and grab them out of the fire. Those who do not share the Gospel ignore their agony in the flames; we know that all must be forgiven or face eternal ruin, and if we do not forgive others and have mercy on them, our Father will not forgive us. Life is short; love is your hope for victory. Be filled and overflow with the power of love, letting it spill into all areas of your life like a bleeding river that cannot be dammed up. Let the Spirit lead your love.

Have no fear for the Lord is with you when you are with Him. It is His Will and Command for you to love all— plural! Above all, love our Father in Heaven, the exalted Supreme Being, and may His will be done that His Holiness be vindicated and may you love your neighbor and love Him, the one true God. Amen.

Hebrews 12:27-29 English Standard Version (ESV)

28 Therefore let us be grateful for receiving a kingdom that cannot be shaken, and thus let us offer to God acceptable worship, with reverence and awe, 29 for our God is a consuming fire.

Focus on love

Listen, brothers and sisters, we have hope; love trusts all. Those who are not made perfect in love think that deception is all around them. For if a man loves his wife or a wife loves her husband but do not trust, then they have not love, but are weakened in fear. I tell you all, do not think only of discarding sin, but think and act on the latter, abounding in love in your sanctification. We need to be transformed, growing in holiness and fighting sin, as well as spilling over in love. We have grown when we love one another to the utmost and love Our Father with all our heart, soul, strength, and mind. Therefore, when you are focused on the sin that is being cured in your life, it is evident, celebrate and praise the Lord with thanksgiving. However, as the Lord tends to the sickness of sin, do not lose sight but focus closely, like putting a thread through the eye of a needle, on the precision of the Lord's tender hand and on the love that is being strengthened and purified in your being, the very soul in which our Lord's Holy Spirit is housed. To God be the glory. Amen!

We always need to keep abounding in love, so pay special attention to your actions and words because love is not sin and sin is not love. Do not be ignorant in this because you know what is good, and the dear Lord will spur all His elect to do good works through love. For justification plus good works equals faith, and faith without works is dead. The product of our faith is repentance and love, which is the fulfillment of every law given under and above heaven. God has put His Law in our heart and infused love in us, and by doing so, we have no excuse but to greatly succeed in holiness, righteousness, and godliness—the very things He has commanded us to be.

Power in Grace

Let us look at the theological principles known as the imperative and the indicative. First, God gives us the ability to carry out His Will, which is indicative of the vital necessity the Holy Spirit has enabled in us, and we are being sustained to that end. Thank you, Father, for your mercy in this and for your abundant grace in our salvation. Being enabled means we were unable, at one time or another, to succeed in holiness because of our fallen nature, our total depravity disqualifies us and disables us, but by God's Supernatural Power that is in and of Himself, He gives us the power to do so, He regenerates us and gives us new birth. By growing in love, crucifying our flesh, rejecting the devil, and turning our back on the popular things of the fallen world, we can succeed, but it all happens by God's Grace, through faith in Christ, and through the enabling power of the Holy Spirit. When I say "grace," I mean that it is undeserved and unmerited; it is not acquired by traditions, but is freely given out from God's Love, the love that enables us to succeed.

God's Grace extended to fallen man

Radical Depravity. Radical depravity means from the top of our head to the tip of our toes, the whole entirety of a person is suffering the pledge and the death of sin. When Adam sinned, the entire human race fell into sin; subsequently, generation after generation has experienced the transference of a sinful nature.

Sovereign Election. If no one can see or hear the Truth, how can we be saved? If on one can come to Christ, even when the Gospel is clearly presented to humankind, who can be saved? The question is how were we saved? How can anyone come to Christ? The answer is "but by God!" and no other way but by God. We say no other way but by God because our salvation is God's alone; it is for His purpose and will. He has given us new hearts, and we are being powerfully drawn into a saving relationship. The work of the Holy Spirit is not just a little love tap that He gives.

Irascible Call. This is the supernatural, sovereign, irresistible drawing of us, whose hearts have been married to lusts of the flesh, out of the world. We are drawn into a saving relationship with Jesus by the Saving Power of God Almighty.

Defiant Atonement. The Death of Christ = The Atonement = Redemption. For whom did Christ die? Christ died for God's Elect, His Chosen Ones. He died for the ones who heard His Voice and followed. The ones whom God's Sovereignty chose before the creation of the world. The ones He predestined and had foreknowledge of and chose before they were formed in the womb. What did Jesus accomplish by His Saving Death? Not one drop of Jesus's Blood was shed in vain. Jesus came to seek and save those who are lost. All whom He died for, He saved. His death was triumphant and glorious. He did not die in vain. He died on the cross to purchase the salvation of all. He secured their redemption. Jesus did not make people suitable; He actually saved them when He died.

He did not make us merely reconcilable or potentially saved from the Wrath of God to come, however. Jesus's death made us reconciled, and He absorbed God's Wrath, but only if we would believe.

The Perseverance of the Spirit in the Saints. The Lord keeps His People right to the end. We, in and of ourselves, are unable to keep faithful to Christ; however, He keeps faithful to us. He has the power in and of Himself to keep us close. When we give our lives to Him, He holds on to us forever, and He will never loosen His grip, even to the last day. The "last day" means the Day of Judgment; our Lord is all powerful and has the power to save all who have been entrusted to Him. He says, ***"I lose nothing" but raise it up on the last day.*** We will be raised up in grace and safely guarded by Christ. He guards us, He keeps us, and He holds on to us from the beginning to the end; He is the alpha and the omega, the beginning and the end, of our salvation. We will never slip through His fingers; none of the elect will ever fall from grace. He will make us qualify and raise us up to a place where we will have full acceptance from God on the Day of Judgement. Focus on love and God's Grace, brother and sisters and neighbors, focus on love and grace. Truly.

Then He gives us the command to love one another, which is indicative, a command that requires not a response, but action. Let me give you an illustration. It is like giving a child a jigsaw puzzle and saying, "Put it together!" God does not set us up to fall by telling us to solve a puzzle that He has not given to us, because God is love. The Spirit He has entrusted to us is an enabler, enabling our faith even to say to a mountain "you go here" and it does. The same Spirit gave Peter the power to walk on water, even though he lost faith. Our Father wants nothing more than to have us succeed in everything holy and righteous; He desires that we have mercy, forgiveness, and love for one another. His hope is that each one of us knows love and grows in love and that we love each other as He loves us and laid down His life for us.

We all need our debts to be forgiven; we have all fallen short of the glory of our Father, so we must freely forgive our neighbors, just as we ask for forgiveness from our Father, and He gives it mercifully every time.

Jesus asks us to love even our enemies and pray for their salvation as well as the vindication of the weak and the oppressed. We should always remember about the poor and the innocent, but the most important one of all is God, who is the most innocent and needs the most vindication from slander and gossip. He came to us as a Humble Shepherd, and He yearns in long-suffering and steadfast love for His creation to be reconciled to Him and not to be like fugitives on the run or scattered sheep wandering around in utter darkness, lost and separated from the Good Shepherd, the protector of their souls. He wishes for us to come close to Him so that He may one day lead us to the safety of green pastures.

His Love is for us, the sheep. God is the most innocent and needs the most vindication from the devil's influence, which can make even the believer indifferent to Holy God. He patiently yearns in long-suffering and steadfast love for His creation to be reconciled to Him, embracing Him and jumping into His Saving Arms with a joyful, rejoicing, praising, grateful, glad, and loving heart. We will praise Him, His beloved son, and His Holy Spirit day and night with awe and a fervent heart.

Focus your love on the Father because He is all in all. Our God is worthy of praise and worship, and He deserves every bit of love we can muster, truly. People who live in love, live in God, and God lives in them. In this way, love is made complete. God must be our center; God is Love and everything that is corrupt and unprofitable that is in His house, which is our soul, needs to be purged and/or eradicated! For Scripture says we are to worship the One True God and no other; we are to love Him with all our hearts, souls, strength, and mind. We are to focus on love and turn our backs on hate.

The Characteristics and Identity of a Christian

Refuge

Chapter 16

The Characteristics and Identity of a Christian

Refuge

Chapter 16

Who do we need refuge from? Does God see His people as lawbreakers who are in the refuge of Christ Jesus?

"Who do we need refuge from?" Well when there is a war or a political division or if the people of a nation or a region are being treated un-justly by others or even their own people or government, and we know that there are other reasons for refuge than these. However, in response other nations and regions make a safe place for the people who become refugees, they provide the resource for a safe environment and especially thee escape from danger. These people are protected, and given aid, and shelter. Many people risk their own lives to protect and give aid and pour out favour on others in danger, so that the people can escape all kinds of evil, relieving them from distress, bodily harm, or even death.

A nation or reign has favored these people in their desperation as there their redeemer from slavery or war or calamity. However, a lot of the time the refugee is sheltered from hostile environments; bring them into a safe environment. They take people to a refugee camp or facility. Therefore, the people are fed, clothed, and given shelter. They are given medical relief as well; we see today that there is refugee support from many governments, and they unite in protecting the injustice of foreigners every day. In our fallen world, lots are rescued, many are rescued from their own people, and countries, who seek to do injustice sadly to their own people.

Therefore, as Christians, we are not being saved from an injustice, for God does no wrong and His Judgment is just, holy, and righteous! God saves us, and we are saved from God, and we are being saved for God and His Glory. Therefore, humans we are being saved from justice! Not injustice! But justice! God's Just Judgment of the morality of our lives!

We are the unjust people and lawbreakers; we have all broken God's Law. Therefore, not one is righteous not one! (Rom3:10-18) Not even the people in the bible where sinless, except Jesus, and He is the only one to ever receive injustice by God. However, it was on our behalf that He received this justice, for He became sin who knew no sin, He died for our crimes, as our substitute. Finally, He raised to life for our justification because His Offering satisfied the justice of God His Father on our behalf as our federal head. This is why Jesus was vindicating and raised to life, death could not hold on as well our God's Holiness demanded that He raises Him from the grave, and ascended Him in glory, therefore, to sit at His Right Hand, for the Lord Jesus lives forever. Amen

We know that if we live a perfectly and continually righteous life and then receive God's Justice we will be rewarded eternal life. For the wage of righteousness is life in this Jesus fulfilled the law and the prophets perfectly and continually, However, living a life inconstantly and imperfectly to the demands and standers of God's Holy Law, then we receive justice, we will be cast into outer darkest where there will be gnashing of teeth. For the wage of sin is death. We are storing up Wrath for the Day of Judgment. Sorry to sound crass brother and sister's neighbors, but our only hope is in the refuge of the Lord, not the law or our own goodness, but the fulfillment of the law and the goodness of God in the person of Jesus Christ. This is our refuge: Jesus' fulfillment of the prophets and the law and God's Goodness and His mercy, for by Grace you have been saved. People who put their faith in our Father's only ordained Way of Salvation which is to receive Christ's Wage, as a gift, our wage is death and all have laboured very hard for this Wage but ***John 14:6 [6] Jesus answered, "I am the way and the truth and the life. No one comes to the Father except through me.***

Our Father is just and righteous in His Judgment, therefore, He is going to judge the living and the dead justly. This is why you and I need refuge.

Why?

Because we all are in great danger, you are in great danger, we need relief, and we all need to escape this calamity from happening. Eternal ruin is the destiny for anyone who asks God for justice as his or her final judgment; such people rely on self, they rely on the God's Law and their feeble attempt to keep the standers of God's Law. Some believe in their own goodness and rest on that "all I have to do is good right!" However, they forget that God is the only one who is good and when we take a measurement of His goodness, it is easy to see that our own goodness falls very short. Then there is man's religion they heap up burdens and moral law but sadly do not come to Christ and fall at His Feet and repent. The very thing we are commanded to do, Repent! We all need the refuge of Christ every day this is not a paper on the benefits of refuge; but it is a call to repentance by faith that we can rest in His refuge in His light. We can come into His saving arms and seek His Will, purpose, and plan for our lives. Because, all who rely on the law for refuge or their own goodness, it is like building a house on the sand, when God's Justice demands a penalty and payment for our unjust words, actions, thoughts, and motives of our hearts we are truly hell bound. The house we have built just washes away. No man or women can argue their innocence every mouth will be silenced on the day of final judgment.

Remember our refuge is in the Father and His Son and His Spirit not in Adam or man or the law or manmade region, but God in the person of Christ through the enabling power of His Holy Spirit. As the representative of the whole creation. Amen.

This is why we as Christians enter into Christ's labour and into the Trinity's saving enterprise. Therefore, Christ gave the commission we must labour in this enterprise of seeking the lost sheep and bring them to Christ to receive redemption in His refuge alone and to receive the gift of life from Him alone. Therefore, He can only give this gift of eternal life alone, for it is His wage to give, His labour did not come back void, by any means. However, perfect and continues righteousness, did He earn. Therefore, we must all labour in the ministry of the Gospel that our labour does not come back void either, but the wage of winning people to Christ will be acquainted with many miracles, gifts, and blessing of all kinds.

However, pray that the Spirit fill you and the heart would find a new love, the love of bring the people to God, to His Son, for refuge, and blessings of the forgiveness of sin. In that, they would come into the light and live in the shelter of God's Grace and mercy upon our lives, this will lead people to heaven. Life lived in the very refuge of Christ, God's Son, who gave His propitious offering absorbing and playacting the righteous hostility God has towards our sin. He gave His precious life in order that we may have new life in abundance by being reconciled to God and not being left as orphans in this fallen corrupt world.

Matthew 28:18-20New International Version (NIV)
[18] Then Jesus came to them and said, "All authority in heaven and on earth has been given to me. [19] Therefore go and make disciples of all nations, baptizing them in the name of the Father and of the Son and of the Holy Spirit, [20] and teaching them to obey everything I have commanded you. And surely I am with you always, to the very end of the age."

We the human race are forgetting one thing... that we have a representative, His name is Adam, He was the first human being He is a historical figure, as is Jesus is a historical figure too. Therefore, Adam is humankind's representative figure and his action have become our actions, the result of his original sin has literally permeated through the substance of man and woman. Since the fall when Adam sinned against God, we know that the penalty for sin is death. Death came into the world through one man. Therefore, the cherubim and the flaming sword blocking access to the tree of life and the result of this original sin means Adams sin has been imputed to everyone account.

So know friend that each of us is a sinner in Adam before we were formed in our mother's womb. This sin has been transfer and or imputed to us all, as a deformity, and we are guilty for Adams sin as well as our own sins. We were conceived in sin, and against God have we only sin and offended and trespassed against His Holy Law alone. Unlike Jesus, whom the Holy Spirit conceived and who was sinless for as one mans transgression brought death into the world one mans righteousness brought eternal life into this world that all may drink freely of the gift of life that is in Christ who gives us His Righteousness that we can stand before God, Justified.

Jesus, was conceived by the Holy Spirit. Therefore, He is not a sinner in Adam. Thus, He became the new representative, the second Adam, for us who believe, this was a pinnacle timer in history: Jesus as our mediator between God and us. Therefore, Jesus is Emanuel "God with us." We know that Adam is the representative figure for the whole of the human race, and sadly he failed by misrepresenting God the Creator where as Jesus succeeded in honoring and glorifying His Heavenly Father, ***Matthew 3:17 [17] And a voice from heaven said, "This is my Son, whom I love; with Him I am well pleased.*** Adam was the first representative of God, as the image bearer, and Adam was the first creation made in the image of God. However, because of His sin, death came into the world; and do to this from one generation to the next humans have had a permeation of sinful nature. God made man in His image. For Adam defaced God's Holiness to the people as His representative, because one sin jeopardized God's holiness, because in the dark there is not light, and in the light the is no dark, sin came into the world through one man, sin gave birth to death through one man, and sin and death produced judgment for all mankind through one man.

In addition, this sin separates us from God and puts us at enmity with God. In addition, God could not be a righteous source of justice if He did not punish sin. God will never wink at sin or push it under the rug, but no, there is a penalty to pay for sin.

Therefore, everyone is accountable to God no one is without excuses the law of God is written on humankind's heart. We are all guilty of crimes against God and sadly, friends we are storing up Wrath for the Day of Judgment.

Therefore, if we do not have faith in the good news that Jesus paid for our sins already, I am sorry for the bad news because if you do not believe in Jesus and His atoning death then you receive justice and the full penalty for your crimes in hell. Sorry to sound crass, but I love you all, and want to pluck you out of the fire friends.

Our Father is Holy, this is His mission to have His Holiness vindicated, and in this, His Word God has revealed His will for us, friends our sanctification. He is restoring the Holiness of Himself, in His People. Therefore, He earnestly desires that we become genuine, holy, sacred, and consecrated representatives of His Holiness in this broken fallen world, leading others to the cross, because of His Grace in our lives know that we can succeed.

If I had a charity and money was coming in and I was the founder and representative for the foundation but after time my staff stolid the money and when they got caught the image of the charity would be smeared and the integrity of the foundation would be subject to disgraced and seen in a different light wouldn't it. I would be seen as someone who corrupted the image of the charity even though my hands were innocent and the staff that is put in the position of head rep would have jeopardized the whole foundations reputation. In this light, God is the only one innocent and we defiled, defaced, and defied His Holiness.

This is the fall of Adam. This is the fall of man. because Adam was the head representative of the human race, God gave him conditions not to eat from the Tree of Good, and evil or he shall surely die. However, he and Eve did just that, and that sin is marked on all humankind in their account in the Heavenly Courts. We all have a sin debt when we come out of our mother's womb and because of this sin debt, we do not sin because we sin, but no! We sin because we are sinners to the core, and in this light the Love of God in our salvation, it is solely in the refuge of Christ Jesus, His Son, that we do not have the hope of being pardoned of our crimes against the Holiness of God. But God has given all He has to free us from the penalty for our crimes that awaits us all: His Son and His Spirit, He has emptied His Love out for us in His great sacrifice, for all He has chosen to partake in His Plan of Redemption, He is the Lamb that was slain, His sacrifice only, satisfied His Justice, on our behalf, for our many crimes and my reply to this and hopefully yours as well must be **"Lord have mercy on me, a sinner!"** Jesus is our Chief Representative. We died with Christ, all who believe, the old man died and the new man lives. To the Glory of God

Adam the one man is our representative, and he was cast out for one sin on behalf of all, however, the next man was Divine and His fruit was life and was glorified and exalted on behalf of all who believe, whereas Adam trade the Truth for a lie and brag death to all, whereas Jesus brought truth and grace and the gift of eternal life to all who believe.

Our, nature is sinful and in bondage and is in debauchery to sin. Our will is in bondage you and me are free to chose what color of shirt we want to wear but to stop sinning we are not free we are in bondage to sin. Therefore, Christ lives rules and reigns in the heavenly places where we who believe are seat with Him, and His Nature becomes our nature we are renewed in the Spirit, we are made new and transformed by the refuge of His Marvelous Word and freed friends from sin and our sinful nature in Christ alone are we truly free to be righteous and holy children of our Father in Heaven.

Jesus as the Chief Representative of His Chosen People, He is the second Adam, who glorified the Head, His Father the Creator and Founder of the whole creation. In this, He vindicated His Father's Holiness, the very holiness Adam misrepresented, as His image bearer. As humankind came in to the world, they were not perfect image bear and representatives of God, but of Adam, because Adam obeyed the serpent not God. Therefore, man's heart is evil continually, not righteous continually, our father was Satan not God, and our image resembled Satan not God, we were proud representative of Satan and sin, therefore, not God and righteousness. We were all children of Wrath not at peace with our Heavenly Father; we were under the prince of darkness and the father of all lies, not the Prince of Peace and the Author of Life.

Christ is our mediator, He represents us and He represents God our Judge. We Christians must honor God and be vigilant in the work at hand, because God is restoring His Holiness in His People that all would be reconciled to God that every eye would see His glory, in His new creation: us His People. That we would bear His Image honourably, represent, and deafened His Holiness with vigilance.

Nevertheless, we have an inability to do this work apart from following Christ we need a new nature, and a living Spirit we need the Holy Spirit that is zealous for the thinking of God. Sadly, we do not heed the commands of God this is our fallen condition we do not believe the one who raised Jesus from the dead.

Humankind is fallen and needs to escape from death and eternal ruin. Our Lord saw our helplessness in this sad condemnation because His Law could not save us. The Law will expose your sin, repent! However, the Law will always leave us condemned friends, ultimately, with the Law, our trespasses grow all the more, nothing could save us, we could not save ourselves selves. For justice demands we die and be cast out into darkness where there will be gnashing of the teeth. So where is humankind's hope: it is in the person of Jesus Christ and the incarnation of God by the Spirit, Jesus is our Lord and Saviour! Our hope, faith, and love are in Him as our faith abides and His hope, faith, and love are in us His People His Spirit truly abides for the greater good and the Glory of God who gave us to His Son to receive redemption, salvation, and deliverance from perishing in the flames. Ultimately, our refuge and shelter that is in Christ, is completely unshakable!

Sadly, most everyone relays on self in the end. Somehow, thinking that we can just do well and we will get justice and rewarded imperishable life. But we sadly forget the sin in our lives. We easily and earnestly forget the severity of our own fall condition as well as everyone one around us, we make our sin small and become sympathetic and callus, and hardhearted! We must flower brothers and sisters, always growing in the obedience in faith. Putting off the old man Adam, putting on the new man Jesus; so believe, repent and be Baptized in the Spirit. Put on Christ, for to live is Christ and therefore, to die is gain.

If you break into a car and are caught, you are then brought before a judge, and the just judge sees the evidence and says, "Guilty!" Therefore, you are guilty in the presence of all under the authority of the court, and then the court sentences you with a penalty for your crime. This is justice! An unjust act requires justice. Equal Payment must be rendered; the penalty must fit the crime in order for justice to be administrated justly. The OT says ***Matthew 5:38***[38] ***"You have heard that it was said, 'Eye for eye, and tooth for tooth.*** This is justice!

Therefore, just think about this; the night of Jesus' betrayal, He was unjustly arrested, flogged, and then crucified and then three days later, He was resurrected and was alive. He walked the earth for 40 days many people saw Him and gave praise and testimony. Then He was exulted by the Father, He ascended in to the heavens and was glorified and seated next to His Father and was given all authority to judge us, He is the only one qualified to be our saviour and our judge, He is Sovereign over life...death...judgment... and all matter. Jesus says ***Matthew 5:39-42[39] But I tell you, do not resist an evil person. If anyone slaps you on the right cheek, turn to them the other cheek also. [40] And if anyone wants to sue you and take your shirt, hand over your coat as well. [41] If anyone forces you to go one mile, go with them two miles. [42] Give to the one who asks you, and do not turn away from the one who wants to borrow from you.*** This is mercy! This is forgiveness! This is the nature of Christ! ***Matthew 5:43-48[43] "You have heard that it was said, 'Love your neighbor and hate your enemy.' [44] But I tell you, love your enemies and pray for those who persecute you, [45] that you may be children of your Father in heaven. he causes His sun to rise on the evil and the good, and sends rain on the righteous and the unrighteous. [46] If you love those who love you, what reward will you get? Are not even the tax collectors doing that? [47] And if you greet only your own people, what are you doing more than others? Do not even pagans do that?[48] Be perfect, therefore, as your heavenly Father is perfect.***

Our Father could not be perfect sources of justice if He did not punish sin. Sin is cosmic treasons against Holy God; He therefore, is innocent in judging us for He created us for His Glory that our words, actions, thoughts, and motives of our hearts would be pleasing in His Sight. Will the clay say to the potter why have you made me this way or the clay say to the potter I am finished? But no! Our Father Sovereign He made us and by the Redeeming Blood of Christ, He has started a work in us, and it will not be complete until the day when we see with eyes open fully, our salvation, and what it truly means to be saved. He created the serpent, and He saved us from the condemnation of His Own Law. Therefore, the justice that condemns us as sinner is applauding to us, who are not in the refuge of Christ at final judgment because the one who receive justice will be cast out like Adam and eve in the fall. Therefore, as well those who denied the Son the Son will deny them to the Father. Those who do not forgive, the Father will not forgive them, and the one who does not love his brother has not been born by God. But those, who forgive even their enemies they will have great mercy and forgiveness from the Father. Truly, Our Father does not seek sacrifice, but for us to do mercy.

Why?

Because we were once enemies to God and graciously, He forgave us all so much. Therefore, we are in need, and He had mercy on us and He died for us in an act of great charity on our behalf and rose for our justification, sanctification, and glorification. "**Thank you Jesus our righteous redeemer**!"

Scripture say we are storing up Wrath for the Day of Judgment. This is a grave danger, we need refuge. Therefore, the whole created order is in desperate need for a saviour. Thus, if we say, we have no sin we are deceiving ourselves and are making God out to be a liar. We need to escape the Wrath of God especially when He has all the evidence He needs against, each of us! So, the question was: **who do we need refuge from?** God! And His just judgment for our lives, He is the Judge, and has given All Authority to His Son, who sits at His Right Hand. In addition, His Son is Sovereign over life, death, judgment, and all matter. Christ is the Judge and when He comes back He will rule and reign and bring final judgment on the living and the dead. In addition, everything is accounted for nothing is swept under the rug; our life is before the face of God, in the Presence of God under the Authority of God, therefore, Jesus came to show us that our lives must be lived out to the Glory and Honor of God. Amen

Be mindful, of our Father, He is there always, be conscience of Him, acknowledge Him in the congregation, in the streets, and behind closed doors. Therefore, He is forever present. Nothing is out of His Sight. Nothing! He is Omnipresent.

Christian, Rejoice! Rejoice! Dear brothers and sisters and neighbors! Rejoice! the Lord is alive He is present He is always present. Halleluiah! May your faith abound beautiful saints, abound in love and patience with a grateful heart, singing to the Lord. Welcome each other, even the people who do not understand the Good news, welcomes everyone to the Lord Jesus is His Name. Abound in love, give justice to all, love kindness, and walk humbly with your God. ***Psalm 62:8 Trust in him at all times, you people; pour out your hearts to him, for God is our refuge.***

Like a tree putting forth fruit, reach for the sky, be like the branches and reach out for the Son, the True Vine. Abide in Him and He will in you, that the Father will see your progress in the Kingdom, and that you will bear much fruit, so proving ourselves to be Disciples of our Lord Jesus. Pray that your strength abounds, that the Spirit fills you and the Holy Spirit protects your tongue, your hand, your feet, your ears, and your eyes from being instruments for evil, but no! Live to the Glory of God; let our hearts be an instrument of the righteousness of Christ and the Grace of God. Thus, we have been freely gifted in Christ we have received His Righteous Wage. Which is life, is it the fruits of His Labor? We must have it, because Christ's Charity is our life, He is Love, it is a necessity to our destiny of being heaven bound, and through the instrumental cause of faith can we only receive this precious gift. Finally, my family be instruments that bring glory to our Father and honor to Him, the Vinedresser.

For Our Father enabled all who believe to pass from death to life, He enabled all who believe to eat from the Tree of Life. He genuinely, out of His great charity and love took the Cup of Wrath away from us, and in His Steadfast Love and in His

Long Suffering, He finally enabled us to be saved. This is why the Father effectually draws us into a saving relationship with His Son, and this is when we did not know we needed to be saved. The Shepherd found the sheep not the sheep finding the Shepherd. Jesus says in ***John 15:16[16] You did not choose me, but I chose you and appointed you so that you might go and bear fruit—fruit that will last—and so that whatever you ask in my name the Father will give you.***

The Lord, He is your refuge... He is your hope... our only hope all of our strength collectively, meaning (the complete human race) must understand one thing: apart from Christ, we can do nothing (Jn15:5) And apart from Christ is where most people are. This is ruin, this is where most people are, in utter ruin, but God being rich in mercy, made us alive in Christ. He chose us, when we did not have it in ourselves to choose Him and He had foreknowledge of us, He predestined us, for salvation in the refuge of His Beloved Son. This was prepared beforehand for His adopted children. Yes, fellow heirs, come into the Father's Joy and enjoy His Life, and His Glory and His Majesty. Seek His Awesome Wonder, awesome, and amazing Love that surpasses all understanding and this Love is for us who believe, **"Thank you Father for giving us Your Son, praise You Our Father and God."**

Psalm 5:11New International Version (NIV)
[11] But let all who take refuge in you be glad;
let them ever sing for joy.
Spread your protection over them,
that those who love your name may rejoice in you.

God does not look at His adopted children who have taken up refuge in His Son and call us lawbreakers, but sinners saved by grace and adopted into His family, His precious people, who were bought by the greatest ticket price: the life of His Son. He said we were lost but then we are found, we were dead but then we are made alive. Then, He justified us, now we are sinners made saint, unjust made just, unholy made holy, unrighteous made righteous. Even deeper we were disqualified from His Heaven, but now we are made qualified to pass through the Gates of Heaven, we were hell bound heading for destruction but now we are heaven bound and abiding in the refuge of Christ's Lordship. We were birthed by natural decent into this world, but now we have been born by God, we have been born again, into His Kingdom. Through faith in His Son alone we have hope friends, we see He is our only hope.

Why?

Because Jesus is the only Ordained Way to God for salvation from the Wrath to come; there is only one way, one door, one gate, and this is Our Lord the Rock. We Christians have built our house on the rock. Our refuge is in Christ and His Limited Atonement on our behalf and lavishing us with the very sign and seal of our redemption: **The Holy Ghost.** We can have assurance as believers that we are His Elect if we have His Spirit because we are born of Him.

We have to know that we were fugitives before we were refugees. We were fugitives from God at enmity against Him, like the rest of the world, we were on the run, fleeing from God, and we were living under the law, everyday being condemned by the law. Nevertheless, we have been redeemed and our sins have been atoned for, let us all come together and walk in love and gratitude for the refuge of the Lord Jesus Christ. Rejoice! ***(1 John 5:11-12)[11] And this is the testimony: God has given us eternal life, and this life is in His Son. [12] Whoever has the Son has life; whoever does not have the Son of God does not have life.***

We need more then help, we are passed advice, we are dead, before we were made alive, we were dead in our trespasses and sins, we were lost on the broad path heading for destruction and God's Word can only birth us into the Kingdom just as He said, "Let there be light, and there was light." Before we were born again, we were walking around oblivious to the hour that awaits us; before we were made alive. We were blind because the veil is over our eye because of our sin; we are completely ignorant to the good news, about Jesus before we were made alive. And all we thought we knew we did not know, with understanding, but had biblical confusion, like me reading a book and you not knowing the content of that book, then me trying to explain it to you in paraphrase, know that all Christian are birthed into the Kingdom of God by His Word and the faith and obedience that follow from His Word, "do not merely be hears of the Word of God, but be doers." So we were all lost, without a lamp to our feet, God's Word was absent in our lives. We were just groping around, like a cow milling around, just waiting for slaughter like the rest of the world. God's Word is the Shepherd's Voice to His flock and He called us to the refuge of His Beloved Son that we can come into a saving relationship with Him, through Faith not feelings or sight but trusting every Word, that proceeds out of the Mouth of God Who is truly Faithful.

Jesus' refuge is our only hope friends, that the Lord has prepared us beforehand a place in the Heavens, seated with Him in the Shelter of His Grace and Protection of His Love, in the relief of the refuge of His Marvelous Light for all who believe Him and put their faith in His Power to save the soul. So rejoice!

We are not being sustained in Wrath like the rest of humankind, friends, soften your hearts! However, we are being sustained, in the Joy of the Lord, who rescued us and saved us from our fallen condition, freeing us from the bondage to sin and being a debaucher to sin. The devil is sly and cunning, he influences us like a lion prowling around looking for someone to devour. Therefore, the Lord's Refuge is secure and eternal, our hope must be in our Lord's Promises to preserve us in His magnificent Grace.

- **Does God see His people as lawbreakers who are in the refuge of Christ Jesus?**

When the Father looks at His Chosen Adopted Children, He does not see us as lawbreakers but Adopted Children that He has set us apart for His Glory and given refuge in His Beloved Son by His Hand. We are being regenerated and washed and given the Righteous Garments of Jesus. He richly and freely clothes us in His Righteousness, this can only reveal the depth of planning and intricate design of our salvation. Therefore, our refuge is in the Lord, if the Lord is for us who can be against us? Not one! His Refuge is our only hope in our desperate state, God in His steadfast love gave us this only hope: His Son. This hope is for all who believe and have faith in Jesus Christ as their Lord and Saviour and when God's Spirit enables us to, we follow Christ and obey His Commands. ***John 14:15***[15] ***"If you love me, you will keep my commandments.***

However, self is selfish and self-seeking, turn inward, not upward, looking to the heavens and the heavenly things. Jesus was from Above we are from below. Yes! And God also is the Justifier, He can have mercy on whom we want to. He can have compassion on who He wants to, He chose us, and He even hardens the hearts of those who are impenitent. We know this, but do we believe it; do we understand His Hidden Will? No! We know what is hidden is for Him only to know, we know His Revealed Will, it is given to us in revelation in Scripture and in creation through the Spirit, but we children know that we did not choose Him, but He chose us, and revealed Himself to us and He never stops revealing Himself to us who believe. In the Scripture, the refuge we have is eternal Christ is the rock and infallible inerrant and immutable with the Father's Promises, that we build our life on, in the Refuge of Christ.

Christ is our Federal Head, all glory was given Him by the Father, the Father has effectually drawn us in and given us to the Son. He brought us in a saving relationship with His Son. Therefore, we know Jesus was not a sinner in Adam, He was conceived by the Holy Spirit. Therefore, He was tempted by the devil just as the first representative Adam was. However, Jesus did not fail as His Father's Representative and image bearer, His Father's integrity was impeccable as Jesus represented His Father, as the God of Heaven and earth, in this Jesus was Glorified and His

Father's Holiness was Vindicated. We know that He lived for our righteousness and died for our reconciliation to the Father. Jesus came and took captives and gave them the gift of life, we were all in chains to the devil at one point in our lives, but the Lord freed us.

1 Timothy 3:16New International Version (NIV)
[16] Beyond all question, the mystery from which true godliness springs is great:

He appeared in the flesh,
was vindicated by the Spirit, [a]
was seen by angels,
was preached among the nations,
was believed on in the world,
was taken up in glory.

Ezekiel 36:23-28New International Version (NIV)
[23] I will show the holiness of my great name, which has been profaned among the nations, the name you have profaned among them. Then the nations will know that I am the LORD, declares the Sovereign LORD, when I am proved holy through you before their eyes.

[24] "'For I will take you out of the nations; I will gather you from all the countries and bring you back into your own land. [25] I will sprinkle clean water on you, and you will be clean; I will cleanse you from all your impurities and from all your idols. [26] I will give you a new heart and put a new spirit in you; I will remove from you your heart of stone and give you a heart of flesh. [27] And I will put my Spirit in you and move you to follow my decrees and be careful to keep my laws. [28] Then you will live in the land I gave your ancestors; you will be my people, and I will be your God.

Our refuge is in His Accomplished Work of Redemption on our behalf. Those who believe, know that Jesus is transforming and renewing and regaining the misrepresented Image of God in us that Adam defaced. We misrepresent His Image even greater but the Holy Spirit is changing the heart, working it over, and softening it, breaking the pride, ego, and arrogance. Therefore, love brothers and sisters, love each other and truly value your love with the Lord Jesus. ***(1 John 3:16-18)***[16] ***This is how we know what love is: Jesus Christ laid down His life for us. And we ought to lay down our lives for our brothers and sisters.*** [17] ***If anyone has material possessions and sees a brother or sister in need but has no pity on them, how can the love of God be in that person?*** [18] ***Dear children, let us not love with words or speech but with actions and in truth.*** We will be a new creation in Christ, not in Adam, but in Christ our solid rock on which we stand. That we can be under the Refuge of Christ our New Representative, the perfect image bearer of the Father and the great commission says we are to be His Representatives, for He is the Federal Head for our Christian lives, He is our High Priest, our High Prophet, our High King, He is the Head of all Authorities, He is the Head of the His Body, and the Church is our

Earthly Refuge.

Those who are new creations in Christ are not in Adam's, but in Christ the second Adam, not the first Adam. We have the Gift from Christ: His Righteousness, we have the curses of sin and death from Adam, but Christ swallowed up death for all who believe.

Therefore, we must honor Jesus' Holy Image to this world that is opposed to Him; because its deeds are evil and all fear that their sins will be exposed so they would stay in the darkness as fugitives then enter the light. The Father is reaching down with loving arms to a fallen corrupt world for you, today come into the Refuge of Jesus and have Fellowship with God Our Father in Peace.

Fellow co-labours in the Gospel of our Lord Jesus Christ, fight the good fight, with kindness, love and Truth, and honor

Christ your Chief Representative...and Federal Head... Chief Mediator ... and Chief Advocate to the Father, the hour of your Judgment is Close at Hand. For us, Christian's have been rescued from death.... final judgment.... and slavery to sin; now live this Truth out in Faith. Go in peace and love one another. Share the Holiness of God, then the Law of God, finally the Grace of God. Thus it is written "the first Adam became a living being." The last Adam became a life giving spirit. The first man was of the dust the second man is from Heaven.

The Characteristics and Identity of a Christian

Discipline

Chapter 17

The Characteristics and Identity of a Christian

Discipline

Chapter 17

The discipline of our earthly fathers is limited by time and by fallible wisdom, but our Heavenly Father's Discipline is planned by His Infinite Wisdom for our good, and He makes us holy, as He is Holy, by His Spirit who enables us to carry out our obedience to His instruction and/or reproof. The Scriptures say, "The fear of God is wisdom and turning from Sin is understanding" (Job 28:20–28), so understanding comes from our victory over evil, our enemy, and wisdom comes from the fear of God's Holiness alone.

Why?

Because seeing God's Holiness will make a man wise and pay careful attention to his own path.

Therefore, wisdom is to know the Infinite Power of God and have this exposed to the heart. We have the infinite in a finite body, who can comprehend this? The Holy Ghost is eternal, and we have the incarnation of the Holy Spirit with us and in us; however, He is in a finite body that is derived and contingent—we are not in a spiritual body yet—a flesh body that is pleased by the gratification of the flesh.

However, the Spirit is pleased by the passion of seeking God's Face. We need to know this power with spiritual zeal, and understand that the path of the wicked leads to eternal ruin, and turn from Sin; it is holiness to choose the righteous way and turn from evil for the Glory of God, Our Creator. Even if we suffer, our suffering is not in vain, because this is being Christ-like. Our Father of Glory created us in Christ for His Glory.

This paper is a call to obedience by faith for believers who profess their faith that Jesus is Lord and are willing to submit and surrender their lives to His Lordship; to them alone is the share of inheritance waiting in the Kingdom.

God's discipline shows that He had a plan to lead many sons and daughters to Glory, which means that the author of our salvation will make us perfect in suffering, just as His Son is. In Christ's suffering, He was grateful, and joyful in the Love of His Father, and wanted all to remain and abide in His Love forever so that we would know the joy of our heavenly Father's Love and abide in it until the coming of our Lord and Savior Jesus Christ. However, He plainly says that we will suffer even for His sake.

When we succeed in the fight against sin, we feel victory and close to Our Father, but when we fail, it is tragic, and we feel far from Our Father; let us come in close and suffer alongside Jesus. He sees us as co-heirs in His Father's Kingdom; therefore, we know that even the Son of God was tempted when He was led into the wilderness by the Holy Spirit. If Christ was not tempted, then how did He have victory; He had to turn from sin to know the temptation of sin and the power of its influence on the weakness of humankind's flesh.

Therefore, Christ was tempted like us in the flesh, but His Spirit never abandoned the Word, instead He used it like a double-edged sword on the devil. However, through much suffering, He fulfilled what we cannot fulfill: the whole Law of God with perfect and continuous righteousness and holiness. Thus, not even Adam could fulfill one command: "Do not eat from the tree!" Adam had a full belly, he had a full garden of every plant and tree, and he had Eve as a companion and helper. On the other hand, Jesus was starving for forty days in the wilderness, all alone with the beasts of the wild. Only by the Word of God Did He have victory. In addition, Adam was tempted once by Eve, he failed, and they were expelled from the garden, whereas Jesus was tempted three times by the devil and succeeded, and after He was tempted, God sent angels to minister to Him and strengthen Him.

Although we may suffer in our fight against sin, the Lord always strengthens us, and the Spirit ministers to us; we are the sons and daughters of the Light, and our Father destroys the darkness in humanity and makes a strait path to righteousness for the one who seeks His Face. This is our power of discipline and self-control: when God wins, we win; when God succeeds, we succeed; and when God has peace, we have peace.

When we read these Bible verses, it is not surprising that all who are adopted sons and daughters of Our Father in Heaven and who follow His Son, should prepare for their inheritance by surrendering to the Lord's discipline. We are disciplined so that we may share in His willingness to make us holy. Remember, it is God who made the plan to make what is unhealthy, healthy; what is unholy, holy; and He is our Great Physician. He could have easily let us stay in quarantine from His presence forever. We are dirty and stained, like filthy rags, unable to be clean again on our own; we need an outside source to wash us and cleanse our souls. We are unhealthy, unholy, unrighteous, unjust, unqualified, unspiritual, and ungodly.

Thus, we do not even blush when we sin in this generation; we are proud and stiff necked, and therefore, we are broken people. However, God calls us a work in progress; He has started to work in our hearts and will not stop until it is finished, even if that means He must discipline those He loves. Thus, if it takes consequences, even harsh consequences, we need to know that it is all for God's will, which is our sanctification.

Thus, all His sons and daughters must be of the Light and not harbor any darkness within His Light, and He is the only one who can fill any amount of darkness with light. Discipline starts with repentance; it exposes our zeal for righteousness to our Lord as well as His Authority and Lordship in our lives. Remember, brothers and sisters, we are all accountable to God, and we can all ask Him to change our heart's desire from the inside for His Glory; this is the workmanship of the supernatural surgery of the heart in the believer and the incarnation of His Spirit in the Christian.

By the Atonement made by Jesus on our behalf, He gave His body as a sacrifice, and by His perfect sacrifice and His life of perfect and continuous righteousness, His words, actions, and thoughts qualified the offering of His life as acceptable for the Atonement on behalf of all who believe in Him. However, humanity offering was not acceptable and only temporally rendered the righteous hostility God had for sin; it was not regarded as final payment, just interest, until the sinless "God-man" became the Lamb Offering, making final payment. Therefore, He did not cancel the debt humanity owed for their sin but paid it in full, and our offerings of the blood of bulls and goats that were unacceptable for final payment, for man's sin, only Jesus' Sin Offering could appease God.

The priest had to repeatedly make a sin offering, but Jesus is the High Priest, and He made the sacrifice for all whom the Father has chosen, once and for all. He will sanctify them by disciplining, re-correcting, teaching, and training them in everything righteous and equipping them by His Word for a life of holiness, godliness, and righteousness. Through the Blessed Holy Spirit and as the High Priest, He makes intersession for us in His priestly prayer (Jn 17) for our success in this fallen world as His disciples.

The reward Jesus received is not a gift, like our salvation, but an act of grace, mercy, and compassion from the godhead. A reward is something earned, Jesus earned His life, and because of His sinless life, death could not hold Him. His death was a victory, and He was vindicated by God righteously and justly even though He took our sin upon Himself and died for us;

justice demanded that He receive His wage: eternal life. His death was not tragic, but it was triumphant, glorious, and truly victorious. Therefore, He paid for the triumphant Glory of our souls and redeemed us for the Glory of the Father's, who gave us spiritual life when we had no life.

We know His Glory is the success of His Plan for His Elect, His Chosen Ones; all Glory is His, and by Grace, we have been freed from hell. By Grace, Christ saved us from God's just judgment; and by Grace, the Holy Spirit has filled us with power and the strength to live by faith and endowed us with fire to enforce solutions and results for our discipline in our Christian discipleship as we walk alone the narrow path. By the Father's special attention, He will guard us, as He guarded His Son—ask and you will receive; if it is accord with the Will of God, it will be done.

Therefore, do not be filled with fear and doubt and laziness that you will never overcome the obstacles and sins that are literally in front of you every day but have victory in the effects of God's Will: that we be, through our Holiness and purity, the salt of the earth, preserving life and bringing many to Christ. That the Holy Spirit be filled in a healthy and holy temple, not defiled and grabbing for debauchery and longing for the bondage of the flesh, the world, and the devil, who is like a lion prowling around looking for someone to devour. Put on the Armor of God, fight the good fight, fight for the good to develop much good, and become saturated in the Word. Become salty and preserve life all around you; your every step should be to serve your brothers and sisters and the One True God and to replicate the Image of Christ.

Suffering and grief was the mark of His Life, so suffer the temptation, the trials, or you should have no share in the Kingdom.

Why?

Because you destroyed the Temple of God, He will destroy you; if the saltiness is removed from the salt, it is thrown away and tramped upon, so if you are defiling your body the very Temple of God, what share do you have with God in His Kingdom? If you are one who hates his brother and is against his neighbor or one who perverts love and defiles the wedding bed, what share do you have? Christians preserve life, nurture life, and protect life, and we are a peculiar people because we are peaceable, merciful, loving, and forgiving of all, even our enemies, just as Your Father forgave all for you. If you do not seek out the well-being of others, even your enemies, then what share do you have with God in His Kingdom, which is pure and rich in love.

The law that God has set before us shows us the level of standards for which we should be striving. We, as Christians, must pray and meditate on God's Word because we must not grieve the Spirit, friends, repent! The Spirit in you is not cowardice but is endowed with power from on high, and the faith He gives us can move mountains and part seas. Therefore, your obstacles and stumbling blocks are but little obstacles to Him who commanded the sun to give light; become disciplined, self-controlled, and as courageous as He is, this is Christ-like.

Die to your flesh and live for God: this is His Will for you in the present moment. When you are with Him, He is with you, and He is here in Spirit to empower His people to be distinguished by love and holiness that by the Love of the Son, He can distinguish and bring His Chosen People away from the darkness in men's hearts. By the love and forgiveness, we impart to others, we show to the world that God's People have a new heart and new nature that is His to give us freely. Among the darkness of man, we live by faith and are saved by Grace; all the elect has received reconciliation and redemption onto eternal life from Christ Jesus, the very Son of God. Do you believe this, child?

In all, I say leave your past sins behind you and turn from the present sins in your life because the future is new and a disciplined person lives in the moment, for tomorrow has enough worries. Live in joy, rejoice always, give thanks to God always, and pray continually. Stay in the Spirit, brothers and sisters, and be alert for the devil because we know that the body is hungry for all kinds of evil, but the Spirit that is now in us is hungry for wisdom, understanding, knowledge, and Truth; your spiritual appetite will grow. The more mature you become, the more you will feed on the Word as though starved; for those who are poor in spirit, theirs is the Kingdom of Heaven.

The way to keep faithful to God is to understand that He is always faithful to you. We are by nature covenant and promise breakers, but He is the Covenant and Promise Keeper. See this and know that you have already been saved by Faith in Christ, not only by professing Faith but also by possessing Faith, which means that you are following Him right now and that you, by the regeneration of your spirit, have faith that God is in your soul; you wake up still loving, trusting, relying, and depending on Him, just as you did when you went to bed. Better yet, this is helping you to grow in a relationship with God, the very reason for Christ's Atonement, our reconciliation, and your redemption. Therefore, you have the chance to get to know God and enjoy Him forever. And have peace with Him for "Jesus is our peace." The Father disciplines and receives those whom He Loves. Therefore, only through Christ, His Son, does He have peace with humankind. I pray His Favor, Protection, and Aid abide in your life forever, peacemaker. Amen.

To finish what I am saying, the main aspect to Christian Discipline is a grateful heart that is filled with thanksgiving and praise. "Thy rod and thy staff comfort me." Without this, we become callus and lose focus on the grace supplied for us in Jesus Christ, our Lord of Glory, who shepherds us in everything righteous. Therefore, if we lose focus on the Truth, our attention becomes fixed on grumbling, which leads to an ungrateful heart with no joy and despair. Thus, we substitute the perfect joy we have in God for the expedient pleasures of our sinful nature. If we have something to grumble about, we will. If we have something to be ungrateful about, we will become weak in our being and despair will enter into our heart because we feel we have no control; a short time later we loathe ourselves and our situation.

However, in this place we seek self-reliance, not dependence on God, who sustains all things, but rather self-dependence, thereby negating all blessings that flow from our Father's Hands to us. We do not seek the Kingdom and righteousness first, but we seek self-gratification and sin to fill the emptiness of an ungrateful heart. We lack focus on the prize and on what God has richly done for us; namely, He has given His Only Begotten Son and cursed and crushed him for our sake—there in no greater sacrifice than this.

Even though we know what Jesus has done on the cross for us, we sin, then we feel guilty for our lack of faith and we hear the devil's sly voice saying, "How can God love a sinner like you?" But through repentance by faith and meditating on the words of grace and forgiveness of sin, the Spirit convicts us and lets us know that we have sinned and leads us to the cross. Truly, as we look up at Jesus hanging there, we understand the power of reconciliation, we have hope in all He has done for us, and nothing else matters except His Love. The path to sin must become less important than the path to our exalted King, who has graciously set before us the path to righteousness, holiness, and godliness.

In addition, as we grow in our zeal for the Law of God, we love Truth and surrender our life to the Truth of Scripture, which is the only rule that binds the conscience in our lives; we meditate on our Father's Law.

Why?

Because we love Him who says, "Those who love me obey me."

God show us we are loved by His Grace, not by the demands of the law. Therefore, Grace is Love and the law is a standard; it cannot give life like God can give life in His Grace. The heart understands the Spirit and trusts everything He says. We grieve the Spirit, by acting in a sinful manner and we grow in grace when we repent of our sin for we are sorry in our heart; thus, we wish we would never do it again, but we know we are weak and that if we were to promise that we would never sin again, our promise would be in vain.

However, the strength of the answer to this question is in the believer, the root. Ask yourselves do you love or hate sin, are you willing to give that stronghold to Jesus so that He is the stronger man who will bind up and plunder the devil who influences sin? Therefore, are we going to embrace Jesus on the cross? If disciplined Christians go to the cross, they will always be grateful. Therefore, the Spirit promises that God has prepared a place for you in this life and in the life to come. Thus, be a productive and holy servant, a consecrated servant, and a sanctified servant. This will have great rewards in this life and in the one to come. We will always live with grateful hearts and spend time planning each day to live life before the Face of God, to the Glory and Honor of God, in the Presence of God, and in the Joy of God with a grateful heart for the grace that God has given to us as sinners

Because of our Father's Son's sin offering that He has made on our behalf, we keep the faith and live through the enabling power of the Holy Spirit, which enables us to do all things righteous and holy to the Glory of God. He can refine us because He is the Spirit of Fire. Refining is profitable so that when you come to the pit or are near a trap, you will not be led or fall into it. You will not be in the dark of the spiritual ignorance of this fallen world but have wisdom from the Spirit of God and be led by the Word of God that is the lamp to your feet in this world of outer darkness

The Characteristics and Identity of a Christian

Bearing Fruits is but by God

Chapter 18

The Characteristics and Identity of a Christian

Bearing Fruits is but by God

Chapter 18

Bearing fruit is our prize and our reward because it all depends on the person God has us become as a Christian, not the idea of who we think we should be. Right now counts forever; friends, think about this, every word and action is documented for the Day of Judgment. Therefore, we are all held accountable to God. So, do you know that right now we are getting way better then we deserve thanks to the great and awesome Grace of God, which is supplied for us all in our Lord and Savior, Jesus Christ? I know the answer to the question, "Why am I getting better than I deserve?" To start, friend, I'll tell you a secret . . . it is a long road to deny yourself and pick up your cross daily and follow Christ (Lk 9:23–24), but along that road, which is the narrow road, the Christian will receive life in abundance, the very kind of life God intended us to live in the beginning: Fruitful. Remember, as we go through this paper, that bearing fruit is not a burden, it is a blessing; therefore, it may be a challenge, but it is not a burden.

Why?

Because a burden bares weight and often yields failure and challenges that are filled with trials and lessons, "Yes!" But these trials and lessons yield triumphs and victories in one's life.

To start this challenge of bearing fruit, we must understand that bearing fruit is not a burden, for the Yoke of Christ is easy and

His burden is light (Mt 11:28–30). The first victory is to master self (2 Cor 4:16–18), which means discipline is necessary and pruning must happen; second, we must grow in holiness—self-denial is part of the believer's life (Lk 9:23–24), which means discipline is necessary and pruning must happen; and third, to sustain a holy and godly life, self-control is a must (2 Tm 1:7), which means discipline is necessary and, once again, pruning must happen (1 Cor 11:32).

Therefore, we understand that to produce the fruit of self-control, which is the scarcest fruit on the Vine, and the other fruits Paul shows us in Galatians 5:22–23, are supernatural, and they are not attained in a moment; however, they are formed by growth and the desire to live a life pleasing to God for His Glory, this is the root of all spiritual progress. Therefore, our hope is in the enabling Power of the Holy Spirit, which gives the increases in spiritual growth, and by the Power of God's Grace, which upholds the universe (Heb 1:3). ***(1Jn1:5) but whoever keeps his word, in him truly the love of God is perfected. By this we may know that we are in him: [6] whoever says he abides in him ought to walk in the same way in which he walked.***

This is the list of fruit that Paul gives to us in Galatians 5:22–23, and Peter and James also reveal to us in 1 Peter 1:5 and James 3:17; this is the fulfilment of the whole Law of God, truly.

Let's look at our text, friends, starting with St. John's Gospel in chapter 15, the "I am the vine" parable. This is a parable about Godliness and the course thereof. Each child of God will grow in Righteousness and Godliness, to the Glory of the Gardener, who is Our Father in Heaven. Amen.

John 15:1-8

15 "I am the true vine, and my Father is the gardener. 2 He cuts off every branch in me that bears no fruit, while every branch that does bear fruit he prunes a so that it will be even more fruitful. 3 You are already clean because of the word

I have spoken to you. 4 Remain in me, and I will remain in you. No branch can bear fruit by itself; it must remain in the vine. Neither can you bear fruit unless you remain in me.

5 "I am the vine; you are the branches. If a man remains in me and I in him, he will bear much fruit; apart from me you can do nothing. 6 If anyone does not remain in me, he is like a branch that is thrown away and withers; such branches are picked up, thrown into the fire and burned. 7 If you remain in me and my words remain in you, ask whatever you wish, and it will be given you. 8 This is to my Father's glory, that you bear much fruit, showing yourselves to be my disciples.

In the teaching about the vine and the branches in St. John (Jn 15:1), the chapter starts out by Jesus saying, ***"I am the true vine, and my Father is the gardener."*** We see that Christ is the True Vine, and we are by nature unproductive, barren, and unable to produce anything in and of our self that is pleasing to God (Gn 6:5, Rom 1:21–25), so the Father has grafted us to the True Vine, who is Christ. We can draw a new extraction of supernatural power, for His Grace alone is sufficient (Rom 6:11–14, Rom 7:14–20) to have us bear fruit.

However, we must consider three main parts in this parable. First, we have no power to be fruitful except from what comes from the Grace of God through Christ (Acts 17:24–25). Second, when we have our root in Him, the Father will cultivate us by pruning us in every way, continually, sustaining our supernatural growth (1 Cor 3:6–9). Third, the Father removes unfruitful, unprofitable, and vain branches so they can be thrown into the fire and burned. Truly, truly (Mt 7:15–20), not one person, especially a Christian, should ever be ashamed to say that his or her goodness has come from God (Rom 1:16–17, Mk 8:34–38) for He gets the Glory in the productivity of our spiritual fruits (2 Tm 2:6), always (Ps 8:1, Ps 19:1, Ps 29:1–2) forever.

The opening statement that Jesus makes is that, "**God is the Vinedresser**." He is the Gardener who owns the Vineyard (Is

27:2–6), has planted the True Vine (Gn 2:8), and, ultimately, cares for the branches to make them fruitful (1 Pt 5:6–7). Thus, the branches are all those who claim that they follow Jesus (2 Cor 3:6); the fruitful branches are the true believers who by living in union and abiding in Christ, have put their reliance and trust in Him, not themselves. Ultimately, the closer they remain to the True Vine, the more they receive God's Special Grace; and the more they remain in Christ, the more they will produce the fruits that are desirable to God. Therefore, the true believer abides in the True Vine and produces much fruit; as Scripture says, the Son is the first fruit (Is 48:12–13, Rv 1:17–18, Rv 1:8) among many. He is the True Vine that came from the root of Jesse (Is 11:10, Rom 15:12–13).

Therefore, the one who has been unfruitful has man's sinful nature and is destitute of any goodness (2 Pt 1:9). Therefore, the only one who has the nature of the True Vine has been implanted by God (Rom 11:22–24), but this is the special Grace of God, who does the planting. He gives the increases to our supernal spiritual growth (Phil 4:17–20), for God is the author of all blessings, planting us with His Own Hand in the beginning with Christ (Acts 3:15). His Grace enables us to begin to take root. We know that man toils in vain when seeking strength in this fallen world (Ps 127:1–2). Jesus teaches us that useful fruit will proceed from none other than Him and the Labor of the Father in the harvest.

God's Grace is sufficient for us to bear much fruit (Hb 3:17–19); it is not us cooperating with God (or the church and us and God) but by and through God that we have been saved! (2 Tm 1:8–10) But by God have you been born again! (Jn 1:12–13) But by God will the branch produce fruit; some 30-, some 60-, some 100-fold (Jn 15:5), but by God! We are the workmanship of His Hands (Eph 2:8–10). God is Sovereign forever (1 Tm 6:15–16).

Jh15:2 He cuts off every branch in me that bears no fruit, while every branch that does bear fruit he prunes Jesus has made two different distinctions between the two kinds of pruning His Father does to the branches: cutting off and cutting back. Jesus says that His Father cuts back fruitful branches to promote growth. In other words, God must sometimes discipline us to strengthen our character and identity and thus, our Faith.

For some corrupt individuals, God's Grace (Eph 4:17–24) is choked out by laziness (Ti 1:12). But the question is will all who have been grafted to the Vine produce fruit? Yes! If they are rooted in the True Vine, they will bear fruit. Therefore, they must have the expectation of Grace and Truth that comes from God's Word of Grace and Truth in order to bear fruit (Jn 1:14–17).

Every branch that does not grow or bear fruit is cut at the trunk (Ez 6:4–6, Jer 50:2–3, Mi 1:7) because not only is it worthless, but also it often infects the rest of the tree (Ti 3:10–11). People who do not bear fruit for God try to block the effects of God's follower, the church, from bearing fruit; theses branches will be cut off (Ex 9:13–16). ***Mark 9:40 40 for whoever is not against us is for us***. In this we must see the believers' need for continual pruning and cutting back in their life. This is the cultivation from the hand of God, and it is an ongoing work of Grace on His part for the branches to persevere, endure, and keep growing (2 Thes 1:3–4), either unfruitful or fruitful. Unless God continues to work His Grace in us, our flesh will abound in harmful vices and will infect the very roots. We need God to cleanse us from all unrighteousness to be a healthy and fruitful branch (1 Jn 1:8–10). When Jesus says we will "bear much fruit," this very parable is the illustration for Godliness; it is the course of Godliness. God, Our Father, has started a work in us, and He is Faithful and will complete it (1 Cor 1:4–9). We will be productive if the Vinedresser continually tends to the branches, and it is the Promise of Our Lord that we who are saved have been reborn and grafted into Christ, and because we have, we will be supernatural in our conduct, our character, and our hearts (Ez 36:22–32). If you keep with repentance, you will bear fruit.

Jh15:3 You are already clean because of the word I have spoken to you. What Jesus is saying is that the ones who the

Vinedresser has chosen have already been implanted in the True Vine and cleansed by His Word (Mk 16:15, Lk 24:45–49, 1 Cor 15:3–11, Rom 10:9–13, 2 Cor 15:18–21). Thus, we have received the revelation of God's love and His Amazing Saving Grace and its depths. Therefore, the Holy Spirit cleanses the heart by the Word of Grace, for this Word of God can only birth us into His Kingdom (1 Pt 1:23–25, Jn 3:3, Jn 1:13, Gal 1:15).

The Lord's teaching renews us, quickens us, changes us, transforms us, and effectually pulls us close to God supernaturally; the Word of the Lord Jesus is sufficient and clear to change the heart as well as to cleanse it (Ti 3:4–8). We are not to live on bread alone but by every Word that proceeds out of the mouth of God (Lk 4:4). For Christ is the Word made flesh (Jn 6:53–58), and the Word of God is necessary to bear fruit—the Word is Christ Jesus (Jn 1:14), the True Vine. He alone is our very source of Grace and Truth that will feed our spiritual life, for He is the life (Jn 14:6).

The physical body needs food, as does the spiritual body. The physical body is hungry for the gratification of the flesh, whereas the spiritual body is hungry for God's Grace and Truth. We feed on the bread of life (Jn 6:48–51), the Truth, and the Knowledge of Grace continually, or we will wither and dry up. We must meditate on God's Word continually so that the revelation of His Grace remains in us forever (Ps 145:5).

Jn15:4 Remain in me, and I will remain in you. No branch can bear fruit by itself; it must remain in the vine. Neither can you bear fruit unless you remain in me. The branch cannot bear fruit on its own. Jesus says, ***Remain in me, and I will remain in you.*** What is truly being said is remain in my Grace and my Truth, and my Grace and Truth will remain in you (Col 1:23). Grace is our undeserved forgiveness, kindness, gifts, and even spiritual fruits that we receive only by the special Grace of God. The general grace is that rain falls on every sinner and saint; thus, as the sun rises and sets on everyone, special Grace is set apart for His elect and chosen. He says that unless you remain in the Vine, you will fall away and become self-reliant, haughty, conceited, prideful, self-seeking, selfish, and worldly, lovers of flesh and money who will have no part in the True Vine. If we abide in Him, we ought to walk the same way that He walked (1 Jn 2:6).

There's only one way to be grafted to the Vine and that is through the cross, our anchor of faith, the beginning of our salvation is in the cross. Grace is only supplied through the person of Jesus Christ and no other (1 Thes 5:9). However, Grace is the very sap that flows in the Vine (Phil 1:7–11) and the hand of God pruning the branches so that they bear much fruit. There's nothing that you can do in and of yourself that will bear fruit (Jn 6:56–58). This is the verse that Jesus declares to us that is the most focused: all who are rooted in Him will bear fruit! They will because they have special Grace from God (Jn 3:15)

Although the Vinedresser waters, nurtures, and protects or even gives aid to the branches, few of them are fruitful, and as we know, all their fruit remains because of God's special Grace of pruning and cutting back the branches that He has chosen to prune and cut back; so all who remain in Him bear fruit, this is God's Sovereign will in the hearts of humanity (Ez 11:19–20).

Jh15:5 "I am the vine; you are the branches. If a man remains in me and I in him, he will bear much fruit; apart from me you can do nothing We are to profess and possess Faith (Rom 10:8–10). All those who are unproductive (Ti 3:8–9) might have professed Faith with their mouth but never possessed faith in their heart; as we say, actions speak louder than words; thus, you will recognize them by their fruit (Gal 5:22–23, 2 Pet 1:5–8)—all who remain fruitless are as good as cut off (Rv 20:12–15, Mk 9:43–45). As we can see, the heart is the matter at hand, for our mouth can say, "I believe," but the heart must be persuaded by the Holy Spirit to have faith in the Gospel Message (Rom 6:5:8). However, this parable is not about salvation, this parable is about producing fruit and the course to Godliness. Christ ***says, "I am the vine; you are the branches. If a man remains in me and***

I in him, he will bear much fruit, meaning we have to be close to and rest upon Christ's Grace and have love that bears fruit that is pleasing and honorable to God the Vinedresser (Col1:5–6).

The last part says, ***apart from me you can do nothing*** (Hos 14:4–9). We are helpless and will not bear fruit that is pleasing to God on our own; the branches are only productive by Christ, not by themselves, only with Christ. The words "apart from me" should mean "except for me." Our Lord is Sovereign, and He is the Authority in the believer's life. His Power is good—it is not bitter but sweet. When you rest upon the Biblical Foundational Principle that He is good, righteous, and holy and that we are all sinners saved by Grace and that He alone has our best interest at heart and desires us to be good, righteous, holy, saints, then we will bear much fruit and increase the Vineyard's productivity. Therefore, the Vinedresser will be ascribed the Glory due His Name (Ps 29:2) in the productivity of the harvest and, therefore, He bears much fruit (Col 1:10).

Jh15:6 If anyone does not remain in me, he is like a branch that is thrown away and withers; such branches are picked up, and thrown into the fire and burned. The elect will never be cut off from the Vine because the perseverance of the saints tells us that we are Preserved in Grace. However, there are many hypocrites among us who at one time followed Christ, but when their hope in the Lord never bore fruit, they became lukewarm and worldly, double minded and under the allure of the devil; they were fashioned in a barren state, seeking after the love of money, which negates the abiding Grace of Christ and nullifies the power of the cross (Is 30:20–22). For those who love this world abide in it, trust, rely, and put their faith in it, not in Christ (Jn 8:47). These people even flourish among the Church, but they never bear fruit (1 Jn 4:4–6) such as love or patience due to unforgiveness (1 Jn 4:7–12); actually, they never demonstrated any fruit; they only preached the Law of God (Mt 23:28).

The branches may be green, even filled with leaves and have the outward appearance of a Christian (Col 2:23), but if we go back to the matter of the heart, when they yield no fruit in the end, it is truly disappointing to the Lord. The time for uprooting is now at hand, to cut the branch off so that it may not infect the other fruitful branches and then throw it into the fire (Lev 26:20–46).

Jh 15:7 *If you remain in me and my words remain in you, ask whatever you wish, and it will be given you*. We are called to ask, knock, seek, and God will give us our heart's desires; therefore, as long as the desires of our heart are aligned with the Father's Will, you will receive His Will. The will of God is found in Scripture (1 Thes 4:3, Lv 11:44); the Scriptures say, ***(Matt 7:7-11)7 "Ask and it will be given to you; seek and you will find; knock and the door will be opened to you. 8 For everyone who asks receives; he who seeks finds; and to him who knocks, the door will be opened. 9 "Which of you, if his son asks for bread, will give him a stone? 10 Or if he asks for a fish, will give him a snake?*** And, finally, in ***(Matt 6:32-33) 33 But seek first his kingdom and his righteousness, and all these things will be given to you as well.***

The Lord sometimes lets us go hungry so that we earnestly pray; the result is that we come closer to Him. He asks us to believe and have faith so that when we ask, He will supply all onto us, and we shall never lack. We always look to the Father's Glory (1 Cor 1:4–9). Christ is our Mediator, and He makes intersession for us by prayer through the Holy Spirit (Jn 17). He desires that we live life and bear much fruit so that we are pleasing to God and remain in His love until the coming of our Lord Jesus, His Beloved Son. He is the one who can do anything; nothing is outside of His Power; with man, everything is impossible, but with God, all things are possible (Mt 19:26, Lk 18:27). The one thing that stops us from receiving anything from the Hand of God (Hos 14:1–3) is our lack of faith, for this will stop the productivity in our growth (Mt 17:20–21). Think of the greatest selfless prayer: pray that in the Vineyard there will be much harvest for the Vinedresser, and ultimately, in your brothers and sisters; pray they are fruitful, and do not doubt, and it will be given to you, for our Father is Faithful and will do it (1 Cor 10:13, 1 Thes 5:23–24, 2 Thes 3:3–5, 2 Tm 2:13).

Jn15:8 this is to my Father's glory, that you bear much fruit, showing yourselves to be my disciples.

(2 Tm 3:14–16) The danger is that those who claim they are living under the Lordship of Christ but become unfruitful and unproductive and who turn back from following Christ after making a superficial profession of faith will be separated from the Vine (2 Pet 1:10–11, 1 Cor 10:12).

Before they ask for the means to bear fruit, they must be grafted to the True Vine by the Vinedresser. Therefore, the Glory of God is due His Name because bearing fruit is not what we do, but it is what God does in the heart of the abiding believer. By enabling us to possess and profess Faith, Glory is due His Name; we abide in Christ and bear much and God gets the Glory for planting the Vine and enabling the productivity of the branches as well as reaping the harvest and giving the increase. The Vinedresser alone gets the Glory for the fruits of the labor (Job 1:6–12).

Jn15:8 showing yourselves to be my disciples In the earlier chapters, Jesus called Himself "the bread of life" (Jn 6:35, 48), "the Light of the world" (Jn 8:12; 9:5), "the door of the sheep" (Jn 10:7, 9), "The Good Shepherd" (Jn 10:11, 14), "the resurrection and the life" (Jn 11:25), and "the Way, the Truth, and the Life" (Jn 14:6) but notice the passage in which Jesus says, (***John 15:1-2) 1 "I am the true vine, and my Father is the gardener.*** This saying from Jesus contains a new element. With these words Jesus distinguishes between the roles of the Father and the Son, for the Father owns the Vineyard and is responsible for its care, its nurturing, and ultimately its productivity. Christ is the True Vine (Ps 1:3) of Israel because He is the fulfillment of the Fullness of the Vine's Productivity of Israel (Is 5:1–7).

Ps 80:14-18

> ***14 Return to us, O God Almighty! Look down from heaven and see! Watch over this vine, 15 the root your right hand has planted, the son you have raised up for yourself. 16 Your vine is cut down; it is burned with fire; at your rebuke your people perish. 17 Let your hand rest on the man at your right hand, the son of man you have raised up for yourself. 18 Then we will not turn away from you; revive us, and we will call on your name.***

It is not that we put on worldly things to add to our spiritual crisis (Ps 36:1–2, Gla 6:3–4) because this world is corrupt (Rom 12:2, Jas 4:3–4) and self-help books, self-help conferences, and meditation are not going to fix the lack of or absence of Holiness and Godliness in our lives (Dt 12:30–31) that we bear much fruit and acceptably worship Our God. But no! We abide in Christ and He abides in us; He helps us live Godly Lives (Jn 15:4–5, Rom 6:22–23) and we worship Him correctly (Ps 29:1–2, Jn 4:24); even further, Christ actually sanctifies us by the enlightenment and revelation of the Truth of God's Grace. God disciplines us so that we become self-controlled, growing in authentic righteousness. Therefore, the exposure to the Truth of God's Grace brings forth foliage in us by remaining in Christ Jesus and obeying the Truth.

Philippians 1:8-12English Standard Version (ESV)

8 For God is my witness, how I yearn for you all with the affection of Christ Jesus. 9 And it is my prayer that your love may abound more and more, with knowledge and all discernment, 10 so that you may approve what is excellent, and so be pure and blameless for the day of Christ, 11 filled with the fruit of righteousness that comes through Jesus Christ, to the glory and praise of God.

However, if the Truth and God's Grace are not affecting the heart, there is no life in the branch (Jas 1:18). ***(1Pete2:2) Like***

newborn babies, crave pure spiritual milk, so that by it you may grow up in your salvation,

Heb 5:12-14 13 Anyone who lives on milk, being still an infant, is not acquainted with the teaching about righteousness. 14 But solid food is for the mature, who by constant use have trained themselves to distinguish good from evil

Therefore, the contrast to the True Vine is our sinful fruits, our wild grapes that are an abomination to His holiness (Jl 3:13), such as **bitterness** (Dt 32:32–33), **natural** (Is 5:2) **selfishness** (Hos 10:1), **deceitfulness** (Hos 10:13), **corruption** (Mt 7:17), and living in the **flesh** (Gal 5:19–21). So, I tell you that you will <u>not</u> succeed unless you abide in the Vine, who is Christ Jesus (Jn 15:9–11), the person God wants us to conform to; the person God wants us to become is the person of Jesus Christ. But the only way we can bear fruit in Him is if God cuts off all the branches that do not bear fruit and prunes the branch that do. Our Father's Discipline is to produce our obedience and productivity; it is for our benefit and growth that He prunes us (Prv 22:6, Prv 23:13–18) to reflect the Glory of His Kingdom (2 Cor 3:14–18). It is for our Glory that we be the Workmanship of His Hands.

When He says, "Be holy because I'm holy" (Lv 19:2), this is His agenda for us; this is His Will for our sanctification (1 Thes 4:3–6); and above all, this is the work we should be laboring in daily. It was Christ's Work, and truly it is now our work, alongside Christ, to fight the prince of the power of the air, the spirit who is now at work in the sons of disobedience (Eph 2:2–5, Mt 12:28).

John 4:38 English Standard Version (ESV)

[38] I sent you to reap that for which you did not labor. Others have labored, and you have entered into their labor."

The Characteristics and Identity of a Christian

Blessed Be

Chapter 19

The Characteristics and Identity of a Christian

Blessed Be

Chapter 19

When we read Psalms and Proverbs it is plain to see that a blessing is a part of everyday life to the people of the Old Testament; it is what every God-fearing person relied on. Whole communities, even whole nations, needed God's Favor, Protection, and Aide. They needed God's Blessing in order to survive just like we do today. Unless we have the good favor of God mediated through His Son we can do nothing, and where we do not want to be is in outer darkness and cursed because if God curses us who can stand? No one. Therefore, if God blesses us, who can stand against us? No one, not even death.

What is a Blessing? In the Bible, a Blessing is depicted as a mark of God's Relationship with a person or nation. When a person or group is blessed, it is a sign of God's Grace upon them and perhaps even presence among them. To be Blessed means that a person or people take part in God's Plans for the world and humanity. Therefore, to be Blessed truly is to be in a Saving Relationship with God, that He saved you and loved you first, that He predestined your Blessing, and that He knew you would have His Blessing. Christian, we have the mark and the seal of His Blessing dwelling in us before we were formed in our mother womb God knew us. This is to have redemption by God's Grace, through Faith, in Christ alone. To be birthed into the Kingdom by the living Word and to be conformed into the very image and likeness of God's Son Jesus Christ, the Perfect Image Bearer. This is your Blessing in Christ Jesus.

The people knew that they either had God's Blessing of Grace, Mercy, Love, and Compassion or they had His Curse of Anger and His Wrath was upon them. This is how it is today, our God is Immutable He never changes; He is the Source of every Blessing.

Ultimately it is His Favor we are seeking. That His Favor and Grace is the Christian True Blessing. For God is the same yesterday, today and forever. He takes no pleasure in condemning to wicked, but He delights in Blessing the righteous, the merciful, the forgiving, the meek, the pure hearted, the humble, the productive servant, the lovers of His Law, and the follower's that worship His Beloved Son.

Although it's common to think about God Blessing humans, it also occurs that humans offer Blessing to God. This isn't in order to wish God well, but instead as part of prayers in praise and Adoration of God. Like when you are enlightened with a heart of gratitude towards Our Awesome God you may say "***bless you God for all you are doing in my life, I can see you. For you are so kind. Bless you Jesus you and your Word are making me holy, I love you, may your name be blessed forever by your people.***"

God Blesses humans, however, this also serves to help reconnect people with the Divine. We know that when we say that our Father is Our God we know that God Our Father says that we are His, He goes even farther to say that we are His Children. This saving and redeeming relationship ought to humble us, our God took the intuitive to save us. And to count us as His Special People, even His Blessed People and Sacred People even further He is molding and forming and shaping us into being His Holy People.

He is wonderfully Holy and Mighty to bless us, Mighty to save us, He is Mighty to do Supernatural Surgery on our hearts and draws us to Himself, not kicking and screaming. He has changed our hearts that they have become softened to the Word and the Revelation of His Word has taken root in our spirit that all who believe have His One Spirit.

Once we all were dead in our spirit and ignorant to the things of God but God in His Great Love made us alive in His Son. We were blind but now we see and see with understanding, Amen. We were deaf to the Truth but now we hear clearly and receive the Truth gladly by Faith. Faith has been a product of the Word. Faith has been a product of the Father's Power and might to regenerate us, and transforming us from the inside out.

We need His Favor, His Aid, and His Protection this is being Blessed having God for you and with you and in you and being one who is as a friend to you. He has given us our first fruits of Faith. Christ is sufficient in Love as our True and Genuine Friend. He is the assurance we have for He put His Spirit in us as a seal of our adoption and a sign of the things to come for the Day of Judgment. Therefore, we are justified by Faith in Him alone, and the very Spirit of God has been placed in us as a seal of that Redemption. This is the Blessing.

Thus the Father has commanded our Faith as well as our Repentance by Faith. We remain in His Blessing, that when we face Him, we are justified and forgiven; not guilty, impenitent and rejecters of Jesus leaving God in the position for Him to have to justly sentence this person to hell, but rather His Son stands true to His Promise of Reconciliation and Repentance by Faith as we as Christian's rest upon the just sentence of our Best Friend and Brother whom bore our sin and took our punishment, on our behalf. Christian, lean on His Righteousness to gain you life, do not rely on your own self. Moreover, we must bring ourselves low and see our need to have a Saviour like Jesus. Because He is the only one to ever be Sinless and be Man Yet Divine. Therefore, the God man, Jesus, is our Remedy, that has the Power to cure the masses. He Blesses us each and every day we are to acknowledge this and submit to His Lordship.

We are the human being and He is the Supreme Being. Therefore, He is seated at the Right Hand of God, all authority and dominion has been given Him by the Father He is infant, from the begging to the end, and whatever God Commands is good. Just as man was created by God as was the animals and the sun and the moon and it was good. God Loves to Bless people with Good and create out of nothing, Good!

It is said that God is Love, for we are all command to love one another and God. This command comes from the Love of God Himself. We are under the Yoke of Christ, and the burden is truly Light, He does not say, "Read your Bible more, be perfectly and continually obedient to the Law, go to Church more, be more religious, practice self-denial more, and you will come into My Blessedness." But no, He says, "Love one another, love Me, Your God, with all your heart, all your strength, and your mind and soul and trust and believe and you will be welcome and qualified to enter into My Heaven; which has been set apart for you my Blessed People!" This is our hope as being Blessed to be embraced by Our Father in Heaven on the day that we are in His Wonderful Presence and ushers us into His House of Blessings. We are His, and we have the Father's Love, forever. This is to be Truly Blessed.

True heartfelt mourning of our sin and the power to forsake them is the fruit of repentance, which always follow after Faith. When we see the Holiness of Our Father and the state we are in as sinner the Father gives us to the Son as a Love Gift, The Son has the Blessing of shepherding us and leading us all to green pasture in Heaven. He has entrusted all to His Son we were chosen by the Father and given to the Son to become a Worship Community that would be Blessed and share in every blessing that is in the heavenly places. That all men everywhere would reconcile to the Father and Love His Son. Therefore, the Father's Plan is that all the people in the dark would come into the Light and Glorify and Honor Their Creator, Their Author, their Designer, and Their Maker! We are Blessed to know the Son, for the Son has life in and of Himself just as the Father does and those how trust and believe the Son and His Promises and rest upon them and have Faith in the Son, He says that He will give the right to whoever believes, to eat from the Tree of Life.

This is a paper on the framework of God's Blessing He has for humanity. Biblically, I am going to study the Bible that I can convey what a Blessing is and a Biblical View, next I am going to illustrate from the Holy Bible who is the Blessed.

We Bless God When We Thank Him for His Mercies

This is how we Bless God by rejoicing and giving Him thanks for all His Wonderful Miracles, His Abundant Grace, and Overflowing Patience, His Thriving Mercy and His Steadfast Love that endures forever, that He has for a fallen creation. We need to be in the Splendour of His Glory, every waking hour Christ has reconciled us to the Father, that we are Blessed through Him and His Mercy to be able to live, "Coram Deo" or "Before The Face of God." We are awakening from the dead, Christian, living life in the full Presence of God, under the Authority of God, the Glory and Honor of God. For Glory and Honor and reverence is due His Name.

That through Jesus Christ we have been enabled through His Great Compassion and Mercy to be Blessed so abundantly. That only through the Son can we can gain access into the presence of the Father and His Love. There is no other way to know the Father or better yet for him to know us, because we all fear Christ saying "I never knew you." As Christian's we want to know Him and become close to Him and be intimate with Him and increase in love with Him right? I hope you want to grow in love with God and His Son and the Holy Spirit? I hope you want to have the Blessing of the Supreme Being our Father in Heaven? That through Jesus Christ we have the Father's deep Love and Blessing. See this closely, do not miss this, we have a Blessing and the Father's deep Love because what Christ did on our behalf when He died in our place on the cross. Therefore, He started the work of reconciling bring man back to His Creator and the renewing the cursed relationship to a Blessed one. The curse that we have all failed God's Law and are all condemned under by offending Him and His Holiness. Ultimately, the Blessing is that Christ died in our place and absorbs our sin and placates God's Righteous Wrath and transfer His Righteousness to us as well as wrought to clear us from all sin and unrighteousness. So the Blessing is that He fully saved us from the law that condemns us. This is why we say we were saved by the Grace of God by faith in Christ alone. So all I can say is keep yourselves in God's Love as you wait for the Mercy of Our Lord Jesus Christ to bring you to Heaven, when you accept this, that is the moment you believe, you have Eternal Life. Though you die, you pass from death to Eternal Life.

God is the one we call out to with Blessings of Praise and Adoration. We as His Children, love Blessing Him. For He is Praise-worthy, we are like soldiers moving forward in rank always guarding His Integrity, clothing ourselves with His Armor. We have been equipped with the Armor of God that is shielding us in the Faith in which we now stand in. We all walk by Faith, and are directed by the Light, led by the Spirit of Truth, for God's Word is a lamp to our feet. The Father's Blessing makes way a straight path, for we have the upper-hand, for we are Blessed in this life and in the life to come. Every day we have the joy that comes from that Eternal Blessing from Our Father and His Son, through the Enabling Power of the Holy Spirit, that our hearts are grateful for the Blessing we have already received and we cheerfully give Blessings of Praise and Adoration to God, whom poured out theses Blessings on us richly; by His Great Mercy and Abundant Grace are we Blessed.

For all the Blessing the Trinity has poured out into our lives this is the small portion of the awaiting Blessing of Eternal Life in a place the Father and Son has prepared for us. Amen Brothers and sisters have joy, you are already saved and in the comfort of loved ones, that we need to know that Our Father is Blessed

Himself, there is no error in God but success is His. Just as Jesus prayed, "Thy Kingdom come thy will be done" we know we can say Blessed be your name when He has foreknowledge and ordains and decrees everything. Even the bird falling from the sky He knows and has preordained it, nothing is out of His Sovereignty or Providence or Predestination. He knows the number of every single hair on your head.

God's Love is directed to the intentions and motives of one heart, and the timeless testing and refining and sanctifying of that heart is to see the Faithfulness of that one heart or to see where that heart lie. But He knows the one He has favor and intimacy for, He knows us by name, He has tested our hearts and His Spirit testifies for us as a Counsel in His Court, His Spirit is the one who defends us alongside His Son who advocates on our behalf. What I am trying to say brothers and sisters is that if you are blessed you are Truly Blessed. The Godhead has saved you and is transforming you, God has regenerated you and justified you and is sanctifying you and at the end, glorifying you, this is our Blessing that we have been rescued from the curse.

First we are in God's favor, and then all Christians have had God's Aid or Remedy applied to our lives in the person of Christ Jesus. For he is the Good news made flesh. Finally, His Protection which is our sanctification that we are deliver and liberated for the devil himself and death has no hold even the weakness of our flesh is freed from the bondage of slavery and the popularity of the fallen world around us that seek for us to conform to it and reject Christ Jesus. The good news over whelmed us with the Truth of Christ and the value for the devil, the flesh, and the world become very insignificant to the glorious amazing beautiful grace and forgiveness and mercy of our Father. It is written, ***if God is for us who can be against us neither death, nor life, nor angle, nor ruler, nor things present, nor things to come, nor power, nor height, nor depth, nor anything else in all creation will be able to separate us from the love of God in Christ Jesus our Lord.*** For the man or woman that have a grateful heart and rejoice and give thanks giving to the one that provided life, as well and spiritual gifts, as well as temporal need, and aw well as the salvation and security of our citizenship in heaven, they see that God Almighty is fully sustaining their life to the very moment of breath and into eternity. All Blessing and Honor we need to shower upon our Father richly, all Blessings of every kind and praise are definite due His Name.

In addition, it is only through His Word that we can know the love of the Father, the person of the Father, the Character of the Father, and the Will of the Father. The Spirit of God dwells in the souls of men and women and by His Mercy we have the chance to fully enjoy God. God forever is the Creator and we forever are the created creatures. However, the ones whom the Father has chosen out of the world, He has given them the right to be sons and daughters, that they have been fully adopted into His Family and are children of the one and only True God and Blessed forever.

So every chance we get to thank God and rejoicing in His Awesome Merciless Wonder that He has done in our lives and the Body of His Unity. When we look at our sin, it leads us to the cross, and we receive the Mercy from Christ. We need to give Him Glory, for His endless works of Blessings and of Mercy that are perpetual unfolding throughout our lives.

We need to slow down and recognize where our Blessing is coming from. That we can exalt God Almighty and Bless Him, Bless His hand for all the goodness in our lives. The closer we get to Blessing God the more grateful our heart will be, the more joyful our lives will get, the more celebrating and rejoicing we will do when we focus on the Goodness of God. The more we look to God and say, "Thank you. Thank you for everything you have done in my life, Bless You Father, Bless You, and Bless You." Because, if we go and lie down and close our eyes and meditate on our lives, we will see ample times when God needed to be Blessed.

We love God, so we care about Him; Christian, Love Him with our entire being, more than anything or anyone. This is not a take, take, take relationship this is a real relationship and in real relationship, we pray and bless those we love and care about. Even though when we Bless God it is not that we wish Him well it is that we give adoration, praise and worship Him for Him wishing us well.

Who is the blessed, this is the big question?

The OT and the NT tells us that the Blessed are the ones who does not walk in step with the wicked or stand in the way of a sinner. The one who does not take the time to sit in the company of mockers, gossiper, slanders and scoffers for the cursed devil is all of these. blessed is to one who Serves the LORD with fear and celebrate His Rule with trembling the one who delights in His Rod and His Staff that bless the undisciplined with wisdom and understanding. Blessed are all who take refuge in the Lord. Blessed is the one whose sin the LORD does not count against them and in whose Spirit there is no deceit.

Furthermore, Blessed is the nation whose God is the LORD, the people He chooses for His inheritance are Blessed indeed; His seal is upon them. Blessed is the one who trusts in the LORD, who relies in the Lord and who rest upon the Lord. Blessed is the one who does not look to the proud, especially to those who turn aside to false gods. Blessed are those who have regard for the weak, for the LORD delivers them in times trouble, the LORD protects and preserves them—they are counted among the Blessed in the land— He does not give them over to the desire of their foes. The LORD sustains them on their sickbed and restores them from their bed of illness.

In addition, Blessed are those who dwell in Your House; they are forever praising You. Blessed are those whose strength is in You Lord, whose hearts are set on the pilgrimage. Blessed are those who have learned to acclaim You, who walk in the Light of Your

Presence, LORD. Blessed is the one You discipline, LORD, the one You teach from Your Law. Blessed are those who diligently serve the Lord, those who endure and persevere in there walk with You; for their reward is great. Blessed are those who act justly, who always do what is right, who are merciful with one another, who forgive one another, who love one another truly and honorably. Blessed are those who give to the Lord's Work, who serve Him diligently, with their time, talents, and treasures. Blessed is the one who is a cheerful giver that proved for the poor and for the House of the One True God. Praise the LORD. Blessed are those who fear the LORD, who find great delight in His commands. Their children will be mighty in the land; the generation of the upright will be Blessed.

Finally, Blessed is he who comes in the name of the LORD. From the House of the LORD, we Bless You. Blessed are those whose ways are blameless, who walk according to the Law of the LORD. Blessed are those who keep His Statutes and seek Him with all their heart—they do no wrong but follow His Ways day and night. Blessed are those who find wisdom, those who gain understanding. For the LORD is a God of Justice. Blessed are all who call on Him and Blessed are those who wait for Him!

The Characteristics and Identity of a Christian

Godly Relationship

Chapter 20

The Characteristics and Identity of a Christian

Godly Relationship

Chapter 20

This is how we Bless God, by rejoicing and giving Him thanks for all His Wonderful Miracles, Abundant Grace, Overflowing Patience, Thriving Mercy, and Steadfast Love that endures forever. We need to be in the splendor of His Glory every waking hour. Christ is reconciling us to the Father, and we are Blessed through Him and His Mercy to be able to live before the Face of God. We are living life in the Presence of God, under the Authority of God, and for the Glory and Honor of God. For Glory and Honor and Reverence are ascribed to His Name and are due to His Name. Through the great Compassion and Mercy of Jesus Christ, we have been Blessed abundantly.

Therefore, only through the Son can we can gain access to the Presence of the Father and His Love. There is no other way to know the Father or for Him to intimately know us because we all, as Christians, ought to fear Christ saying, **"I never knew you."** So we want to know Him as Our Lord, become close to and intimate with Him, and increase our love for Him right now, don't we? I hope you want to grow in love with God and His Son and the Holy Spirit. I hope you want to have the Blessing of the Father, the Supreme Being, in Heaven. Through Jesus Christ we have the Father's Deep Love and Blessing. See this closely and do not miss this: We are Blessed by the Father's Deep and Unfailing Love.

Because Christ, on our behalf, died on the cross, He started the work of reconciling man to Him and our Holy Father and reversing the cursed relationship to a Blessed One. The curse is that we failed Law and are all condemned under it, but the Blessing is that Christ died in our place and absorbed our sin and God's Wrath and transferred His Righteousness to us and cleared us from all sin. He is sanctifying us and making us become righteous and holy men and women. "O, come Emmanuel!" So the Blessing is that He fully saved us from the law that condemns us. Yes, this is why we say we were Saved by the Grace of God and by faith in Christ alone. However, all I can say is keep yourselves in God's Love as you wait for the mercy of Our Lord Jesus Christ to bring you to Heaven.

The moment you believe; you have Eternal Life. And although you die, you pass over to life. The Lord has given you the Promised Holy Spirit and Seal of Your Redemption, and the King has put His Mark on you and deposited the Holy Spirit in you. God is the one we call to with Blessings of Praise and Adoration. We, as His Children, love and Bless Him because He is Praiseworthy. We are like soldiers moving forward in rank; we always guard His integrity, clothing ourselves with the Righteous Armor of God. We have been equipped with the Armor of God, which shields us in the Faith in which we now stand.

In everything we walk by Faith, and we are directed by the Light, and we are led by the Spirit of Truth. The Father's Blessing makes way a straight path, and we have the upper hand because we are Blessed in this life and in the life to come. Every day we have the joy that comes from our Father and His Joy. Through the enabling Power of the Holy Spirit, our hearts are grateful for the Blessing we have already received, and we cheerfully give blessings of praise and adoration to God, who has poured the Blessings of His Great Mercy and Abundant Grace on us.

For all the Blessings the Trinity has poured into our lives, this is but a small portion of the awaiting Blessing of Eternal Life in a place the Father, Son, and Holy Ghost has prepared for us. Amen.

Brothers and sisters, rejoice that you are already saved and take comfort in loved ones. We need to understand that our Father is Blessed Himself; there is no error in God, but success is His. Just as Jesus prayed, "Thy Kingdom come Thy Will be done," we know we can say, "Blessed be Your Name," when He has foreknowledge and has Ordained and Decreed everything in His Sovereign Power. Every bird that falls from the sky, He knows of and Preordained it; nothing is out of His Sovereignty or Providence. He has numbered every single hair on your head. His love is directed to the intentions and motives of one's heart.

Therefore, the timeless testing, refining, and sanctifying of that heart is to test the Faithfulness of that one heart; He intrudes on the heart to see where that heart lies. But He knows the ones He has favor and intimacy with—He knows us by name. The Lord has tested our hearts, and His Spirit testifies for us as a Counselor in His court. His Spirit is the one who defends us alongside His Son, who advocates on our behalf. God knows the whole complete inner condition; nothing is hidden from the Eyes of God, not even the hearts of men. What I am trying to say here, brothers and sisters, is that if you are Blessed, you are Truly Blessed. The Godhead has saved you and is transforming your sanctification. God has regenerated and justified you and is sanctifying you, and at the end, He will glorify you. We have been rescued from the curse.

First, we receive Favor, all Christians have. Next, we receive God's Aide, the Remedy is applied to our lives through the personal work of Christ Jesus—He is the Good News. Finally, His protection, which is our sanctification, delivers and liberates us from the devil himself, and death has no hold on us, even the weakness of our flesh is freed from the bondage to and debauchery of the fallen world, which tries to make us conform to it and reject Christ. But Jesus overwhelms the darkness with the Truth of the Light.

The value of the devil, the flesh, and the world becomes insignificant to the glorious, amazing, and beautiful forgiveness and mercy of Our Dear Father. It is written in the Scripture: ***"if God is for us who can be against us neither death, nor life, nor angel nor ruler, nor things present, nor things to come, nor Power, nor height, nor depth, nor anything else in all creation will be able to separate us from the love of God in Christ Jesus our Lord."*** For the man or woman who has a grateful heart and rejoices and give thanks to the one who has provided life, as well as spiritual gifts and the salvation and security of our citizenship in Heaven, sees that God Almighty is fully sustaining his or her life to the last moment of breath and into eternity. We need to shower all blessing and honor upon our Father; all blessings of every kind and praise and adoration are definitely due His Name.

Know God

In addition, it is only through His Word that we can know the Love, the Person, the Character, and the Will of the Father. The Spirit of God dwells in the souls of men and women, and by His mercy, we have the chance to fully enjoy God. God is forever the creator, and we are forever the created creatures. However, the ones whom the Father has chosen out of the world He has given the right to be sons and daughters; they have been fully adopted into His family and are children of the one and only True God. So every chance we get, we must thank God and rejoice in the awesome merciful wonders that He has done in our lives. When we look at our sin, it leads us to the cross, and we receive Mercy from Christ. We need to give Him Glory for endlessly revealing His works of Blessing and Mercy that are perpetually unfolding throughout our lives. We need to slow down and recognize where our Blessings are coming from. That we can exalt God Almighty, Bless Him, and Bless His hand for all the goodness in our life. The closer we get to Blessing God, the more grateful our heart will be, the more joyful our lives will get, and the more celebrating and rejoicing we will do when we focus on the Goodness of God.

The more we look to God, the more we will say, "Thank You. Thank You for everything You have done in my life; Bless You, Father, Bless You." Because if you go and lie down and close your eyes and meditate on your life, you will see ample times when God needed to be blessed; we love God, so we care about Him. We love Him with our entire being, more than anything or anyone. This is not a take, take, take relationship; this is a real relationship, and in a real relationship, we pray and bless those we love and care about. Even though when we bless God it is not that we wish Him well, it is that we adore, praise, and worship Him because He wishes us well.

We have the Blessing of the Holy Trinity

We have the Blessing of the Holy Trinity. Jesus has come on a mission to save all that the Father has given Him. There is perfect unity within the Godhead: The Father, The Son, and The Holy Spirit. The Son came to seek and to save the ones the Father chose to give Him. The number one reason we need to believe in the Atoning Death of Christ is the perfect unity of the Godhead and that there is one plan of redemption, one purpose to bring lost sinners to Christ for salvation, and one will to bring Glory and Honor to God and enjoy Him forever. The unity of the Godhead (God the Father, God the Son, and God the Holy Spirit) works together in perfect harmony, in one saving purpose, and in one saving enterprise to save sinners. It is all by the Father's Love that we have been saved. The Trinity never pulls in opposite directions; they never work in contrary purposes to each other. That is what Jesus is saying here. He is saying that He is not coming to be contrary to the Father, but to do His Will. Also, when He says, "I and the Father are one," what He is saying is that the Trinity has a will and a purpose to save us, and we must have the same will and purpose as the Triune God we follow or we will contradict Him and His Will and purpose. The Grace and Love of the Trinity is beyond our understanding, but Scripture says, "And everyone who thus hopes in Him purifies himself as He is pure." Come, purify yourself. Remember, there is no love greater than the love of Christ's sacrifice on the cross.

NIV John 10:30
30 I and the Father are one."

John 6:38 New International Version (NIV)

[38] For I have come down from heaven not to do my will but to do the will of him who sent me.

The Characteristics and Identity of a Christian

We Need to Call on the Lord, Period

Chapter 21

The Characteristics and Identity of a Christian

We Need to Call on the Lord, Period

Chapter 21

We need to call on the name of the Lord because we are called to trust Him, rely on Him, and rest upon Him alone. We need His Blessing because the highest state in life is to be Blessed by God and to be in God's Favor and to receive His Aide and Protection. We are called to surrender our will to Our Lord God. We know how much we love God when we see to what degree we carry out His Will.

We are to love God with our entire being. The Lord calls the lost, the blind, and the sinners; He gathers them and teaches them the Truth about the Good News through His prophets, the disciples, the evangelists, and the apostles; they are the official ambassadors of the Word of God, the Father.

Christ's Irresistible Call to Grace reaches the lost sinner and the spiritually dead and blind so that they are found; He seeks the ones who are dead in sin that they may live through His Righteousness. Before we believed, we were all spiritually blind, but now we see. We were lost but now we are found. We were dead but now we are made alive. This is the power of the Gospel! In the Gospel the Lord called us to Him. And we, as His Chosen People follow, for the call to Grace and Salvation is irresistible to the Chosen People of God.

In this paper, we will see that the need for a relationship with Christ is a necessity. We need to call on the Lord for a myriad of health needs, spiritual gifts, and temporal needs for our sustenance. The Lord calls on us to Glorify Him, Obey Him, Worship Him, Serve Him, and Enjoy Him forever. The list is abundant. However, as we read, we see the devil's calling is for us to follow the desires of our flesh, and the result is that we follow the worldly system. The devil and the weakness of our flesh lead us to death and to destruction. In this paper, the main theme is that we are called to abandon all hope from the world and to call on the Lord, period. We are to learn what the Lord's Calling is for each of us in our lives.

We are called by the Lord to listen to God's Word, which has come through the prophets, the disciples, the evangelists, and the apostles from our High Priest Jesus Christ. These are the Official Ambassadors of the Word of God.

The first list that we a going to look at is what the Lord is calling us to. Above all, we are called to mirror and reflect the Holiness of God. We are all called to believe and put our faith in our Lord, Jesus is His Name. We are called to model Christ to our neighbor. This means we are to conform to the Will of God so that people can actually look at us and see the reflected Glory of God in our lives. By walking in Faith, we will see that we are called by the Name of the Lord in everything holy in love, mercy, and peace. God's Spirit puts forward Light that will shine in our lives; God's Light will be impossible to hide. The force of God's Spirit will be unmistakably transforming for our lives.

Next, the Lord Blesses all who come in His name and who openly profess that Jesus is Lord, so the Lord calls us to profess our Faith. We are called to speak from the Holy Spirit so that we will have confidence in promoting the Gospel Message and promoting the fame of Jesus Christ in all aspects of our life. We are called to put our Faith into action since Faith without deeds is dead. We are to choose the Christian life as a Calling for a big reason: It is so we and our children may live life abundantly and eternally and so we may prosper in the richness of God's Grace, which is supplied for us in His Blessed Son, Jesus Christ.

Lastly, if we do not do what God is Calling us to do, we will be led not to life, but to death; our existence will not be Blessed but cursed. In this chapter, I am going to illustrate in the form of lists how important it is that we call on the Lord and how the Lord calls on us. We will also see how we are affected by the call of humanity and of the devil, leading us to follow the desires of our flesh and to submit to this fallen world system.

(NIV®.) Deuteronomy 18:19 New International Version (NIV)

[19] I myself will call to account anyone who does not listen to my words that the prophet speaks in my name

Luke 18:16-17New International Version (NIV)

[16] But Jesus called the children to him and said, "Let the little children come to me, and do not hinder them, for the kingdom of God belongs to such as these. [17] Truly I tell you, anyone who will not receive the kingdom of God like a little child will never enter it."

The Lord calls upon us daily. He speaks to us through His Word. His lips speak the infallible and immutable Truth to us; He is the Voice of Peace, Truth, Reason, Logic, and Authority. His Hands stretch out to embrace us, comfort us, strengthen us, and empower us. He shows us His Love and Compassion when we are walking with the Lord. He is with us; that is why we are to remain and Abide in Him. He will remain in us as we remain in Him.

Therefore, the Lord is Mighty, "All Powerful," and slow to anger. The Lord calls upon us to hate sin and to turn from them so that we will follow Him and deny the devil, our flesh, and the world. When I say the world, I mean the fallen nature around us. When I say the flesh, I mean fallen humanity. When I say the devil, I mean the fallen spirit who is now at work in those who are disobedient and rebellious.

The Lord calls us to obey Him because He does not take pleasure in condemning the wicked at all; He does not even take pleasure in punishing or disciplining His Beloved People, but He Loves us all, and He calls us all to repentance so that we may be forgiven, live, and not perish in our sin. The Lord calls us to penitence for our sin; He calls us to grieve and mourn over the wrongs that we have done. Many people in the Bible wore sackcloth and ashes as a public display of extreme grief, remorse, or repentance.

(NIV®.) ***Luke 5:32 New International Version (NIV)***

32 I have not come to call the righteous, but sinners to repentance."

The Lord calls us to believe the Message of the Gospel, but on one hand, we must call on the Lord ourselves because this is reliance, and the Lord is our Shepherd; therefore, it has been the action of humankind to refuse to heed the Call. In our distress and, most of the time, desperation, humanity refuses to call upon the Lord.

As Christians, we need the Lord to protect us, to give us aide, to sustain us, to bless us, and to preserve our lives. We need to call on the Lord to deliver us from the evil of others, to rescue us, to take us out of oppression, and to lead us away from the entrapment of sin. We need to call on the Lord to help us fight sin, temptation, and the devil himself. We need to call upon the Lord to sustain our life when we feel like there is no hope. We need to call on Him to feed us, clothe us, and shelter us. We need to call on the Lord for our temporal needs, to give us clean water to drink, warmth, and light. The whole world and everything in it needs to know that we are mirror creatures and our Lord God is the Creator of the Heavens and the earth and all things good for His Glory. We are the creature; He is the Creator, and He sustains life.

(NIV®.)2 Samuel 22:5-7 New International Version (NIV)

***[5] The waves of death swirled about me;
the torrents of destruction overwhelmed me.
[6] The cords of the grave coiled around me;
the snares of death confronted me.***

***[7] "In my distress I called to the LORD;
I called out to my God.
From his temple he heard my voice;
my cry came to his ears.***

We are to call on the Lord in distress to pull us out of poverty, to send water on our crops, and to stop destruction from coming on our land. We call on the Lord to rescue us from earthquakes, tsunamis, tornadoes, hurricanes, fires, and floods. We are to call on the Lord to stop famine, plagues, sickness, disease, and death.

We need to call out to the Lord in our desperation to save us from our enemies and to help us when we go into battle or when we seek for the missing or the abducted. We are to call upon the Lord to receive our dead, to give good health to the newborn, and to give good heath to us and others.

We should call on the Lord to give us victory in sports or in any of our challenges. We must call on the Lord to drive out evil, to bring the wickedness of people to account, and to free us from our slavery to sin and debauchery so that we can be liberated from our bondage. We call upon the Lord to bring our actions to account; we need to call out for mercy, justice, grace, and help.

Finally, at all times we need to call on the Lord; we need His powerful comfort and His Mighty Outstretched Hands to help us, guide us, counsel us, and discipline us so that we can have hope. There are thousands of more things that we can call on the Lord for and thousands of things we need to call on the Lord for.

Why?

Because, truly, I tell you there is no one to hear us, no one to listen to us, and no one to answer us besides the Lord God. His Heart is Pure and Holy, and He listens to whoever comes to Him with a humble heart, to all who know he or she are sinners and who Exalt and Glorify the Supreme Deity and Authority of Our Sovereign Lord, Jesus Christ.

(NIV®.) ***Psalm 3:4 New International Version (NIV)***

[4] I call out to the LORD,
and he answers me from his holy mountain.

(NIV®.) ***Psalm 4:3 New International Version (NIV)***

[3] Know that the LORD has set apart his faithful servant for himself;
the LORD hears when I call to him.

(NIV®.) ***Psalm 17:6New International Version (NIV)***

[6] I call on you, my God, for you will answer me;
turn your ear to me and hear my prayer

Now we will look at what the Lord calls us to call on Him for. The Lord asks us to call on Him for wisdom, knowledge, understanding, guidance, direction, stability, long life, and prosperity; we are to call out for faith and Truth. We need to call on the Lord so that we may not be put to shame, be falsely convicted, or be judged unjustly. We also are asked to call upon the Lord for our vindication. We are asked to call out to the Lord so that we are never led astray and that we never stop learning from His Word but continue to be motivated to pursue Him and His Will. We are asked to call out to the Lord for clarity and enlightenment, to open our eyes so that God's Word is revealed to us in its depth of understanding. We are asked to call out and pray for spiritual sight, spiritual gifts, and spiritual fruits for ourselves and for our brothers and sisters so that we all receive them.

We are asked to call on the Lord to continue revealing His Will, His Word, and Himself to us so that we can know His Nature, His Character, and His Person better every day. As Christians, we are asked to call on the Name of the Lord because we are instructed to be set apart from this world. But first we need to know what God is calling us to do so that our lives are separated from the world.

(NIV®.) ***Psalm 50:15 New International Version (NIV)***

[15] and call on me in the day of trouble;
I will deliver you, and you will honor me."

The Lord commands us to assemble as His Body, the Church, to unite and become reconciled to God the Father and to be good stewards. The Lord directs us to Obey His Commands; we are called to be obedient to His Word, forgiving, and merciful to others. He commands us to love one another and to be guided by His Almighty Truth. We are called by the Lord to Jesus Christ, Our Lord, and to repent of our sin by faith.

We are commanded to serve, to heal, to build up the Church, and to give remembrance to the Lord's Day. We are to remember what the Lord has done for us all. We are called to bless people and to sincerely pray for their protection, aid, and God's Favor to be on them. Christ paid the price for our debt on the cross; He ransomed us from the punishment of death. We are commanded to keep the Lord's Day holy.

The Lord commands us to keep order among ourselves; we are commanded to worship the Lord, to sing songs of praise and to honor Him. We are called to sing the Bible, pray the Bible, speak the Bible, read the Bible, hear the Bible, and see the Bible through the Holy Sacraments of Baptism and the Lord's Supper.

We are commanded to have very high regard for the Lord, give reverence to Him, and exalt Him as the Highest. We are called to trust the Lord, to rely on Him, to depend on Him, to put our faith in Him, and to rest in Him solely. There is no love greater than the love of the Lord; to believe in Him, to know Him, to listen to Him, to respect Him, to fear Him, and to love Him are gifts given by God. Once again we are commanded to worship the Lord God by singing, praying, preaching, reading, and studying the Holy Bible. We are called to see His Authority and to submit to it by our will and to submit to His Rule and Government by our will; we are commanded to give thanks to the Lord in all circumstances. We are called to surrender to Him and fully live for Him through His Will; we are commanded to have a relationship with Him and to pray without ceasing.

He commands us to be sober-minded. We are to teach the little ones to Believe in Him, to Serve Him, to Submit to Him, and to become malleable to His Teaching. We are to raise our children in the culture of the Holy Bible, as Christ intended. The Lord commands us to Righteousness, Holiness, and Godliness. We are not to merely feel these words, but we are to live and act on God's Commands, as the Way of life.

As Christians, we are to invest the time, talents, and treasures that the Lord has given us so that we can have the chance to give something back to His cause, with the hope of promoting the fame of Jesus Christ and of magnifying the glorified God Almighty. Remember that the Lord loves a cheerful giver, so we, as Christians, need to give and to live a life of charity. As Christians, we need to be good stewards. We are all called to serve God and to tell others about Him. As Christians, we need to share the love of Jesus Christ with the world. Any chance we get we need to share the Truth of the Gospel in the hopes of plucking another soul from the fire. Laypersons are not called and commissioned to preach the Gospel as His ambassadors, but all Christians need to serve others in the name of Jesus Christ and share the message of Eternal Salvation.

We need to share Christ's Perfect Life of righteousness, holiness, blamelessness, and to be free of sin. We need to share the miracles and the work that He performed. We need to share His Atoning Death and the propitious sacrifice that He made on our behalf on the cross. As Christians, we need to tell people about the death, burial, resurrection, and ascension of Jesus Christ. We need to desperately inform our friends, our family, and strangers about the love of Christ and of God the Father, the love that He has for a fallen creation. His love has long stranded since before the creation of the world.

As Christians, we need to take part in communion with the Lord, in remembrance of what He did on the cross. As Christians, we need to study God's Word and ask that God will reveal His Calling to us. However, above all, we need to have Faith and Believe; we need to change our image and become conformed to the person of Jesus Christ that is revealed to us in the Scriptures. In all that we do, we are to love God with all our strength, all our mind, and all our heart, loving one another as we love ourselves. Amen.

(NIV®.) Micah 6:9 New International Version (NIV)

9 Listen! The Lord is calling to the city—
and to fear your name is wisdom—
"Heed the rod and the One who appointed it.

(NIV®.)2 Chronicles 7:14 New International Version (NIV)

14 if my people, who are called by my name, will humble themselves and pray and seek my face and turn from their wicked ways, then I will hear from heaven, and I will forgive their sin and will heal their land.

Lastly, the devil calls humanity to live in a certain way as well and he tries to direct our calling. The sad thing is that the devil calls human hearts to murder, lie, steal, assault, rape, and pillage one another. The devil calls the human heart to prostitute itself and enslave itself in addiction. The devil calls our human hearts to inflict pain and suffering and to invoke mistrust in one another. The devil calls our human hearts to worship false gods and idols, to pursue ungodliness, and to live a life in rebellion and defiance.

He calls us to live a life that contradicts and opposes God. The devil calls the human heart to cheat, give false testimony, slander, and gossip. The devil calls our human hearts to a life of hostility, revenge, discord, confusion, and delusion! The devil calls our human hearts to jealousy, prejudice, greed, vanity, and ill-gotten gain. The devil calls humanity to disobedience, depravity, war, oppression, force, control, defiance, dishonor, rage, envy, hate, hate crimes, hostility, and offenses against God.

The devil calls humanity to genocide, punishment, cosmic treason, plotting and conspiring with evil, and sexual immorality. The devil calls human hearts to child abduction, kidnapping, torture, lawlessness, intoxication, inebriation, and violence. The devil calls our hearts to adultery, perversion, witchcraft, pornography, and an unhealthy way of life. Finally, the devil calls human hearts to sin, sin, sin, sin!

We can look at this list of wickedness and evil and be certain that there is much more we could add. So do not think humanity has enabled itself to do anything righteous. We are on our own in this mess; to turn things around we need to have help from God the Father, from Jesus the Son, and from the Holy Spirit. We are not called to live as we see fit, for our own ways are evil. Instead, we are to listen to every Word that proceeds from the mouth of God. We need to listen to what God is calling us to do, period!

We need to do what is right and just in His eyes. We ought to do things God's way, not ours, because if we just do as we see fit and if we do things by our standards, the human race will just walk farther away from what God wants and from what He is calling us to. The sad thing is that in the end, we will just have to suffer the consequences for our actions. Without the Lord's Light in this world, it would be a very dark place indeed.

I pray that He keeps the floodwaters at bay so that they do not wash us away. It is sad, but as humans, our minds are perverse; we are all self-seeking and, initially, without understanding; we are all slaves to our own sin. Sorry to say, but every human, by nature, is in this fallen state; I tell you, not one is holy. No one is righteous by his or her own merits; we are all in a state of confusion. God is our Guide. He has always been our Guide. So when He calls on you, answer, because when you call on Him, He always hears. Fight the devil! Jesus always gives us a door to go through; we just need to enter it—sometimes we just need to knock. And by Faith, every sin has an exit; there is always an open door of escape.

Our God loves to see us succeed in righteousness. Jesus always offers a way out. Just listen, open your heart, open your mind, and open your ears. Jesus liberates every one of us out of bondage and debauchery. We can only serve one master: Satan and sin or God and righteousness.

The Characteristics and Identity of a Christian

Sanctification

Introduction

Chapter 22

The Characteristics and Identity of a Christian

Sanctification

Introduction

Chapter 22

Successful growth in our sanctification will happen in five essential elements. First, we need the renewal of our mind (Rom 12:2). Second, we need Sound Doctrine (1 Tm 4:16). Third, we need the Sanctification that can only come from the Truth of God's Word (Jn 17:17). Fourth, we are all Sanctified by the Faith we have for Christ (Jn17:17–19), and fifth, we need the Holy Spirit's Truth to convict us, show us that we are sinners, and lead us to Repentance by Faith so that we may know and desire Truth. Therefore, so that Truth will be a way of life in the Spirit of the Children of God, forever (2 Thes 2:13). Ultimately, we need the Power of the Holy Spirit to advance all growth; without Him, we are powerless to push forward and enter into the Kingdom. Therefore, we are without any hope on our own to grow or to succeed in righteousness, holiness, and godliness (Jn 15:4–5). Even as mature Christians, we are too weak; therefore, we can do nothing (Jn 15:5) unless we are enabled to do so by the Might of the Holy Spirit and the Truth and Grace from Jesus Christ (Jas 1:18). This paper is a brief introduction to Sanctification, talking about the difference between Justification and Sanctification as well as our need for a covering and washing of sin.

In addition, I have not believed anyone who says that he or she can Sanctify him- or herself before the Face of God Almighty (Jas 3:1–12). Thus, the purification of the soul and the heart comes from and through obeying the Truth (1 Pt 1:22) of God's Holy, Sacred, Immutable, Inerrant, and Infallible Word through Christ Jesus (Jn 15:3). There is no other way; we cannot be Sanctified in a lesson with five steps; sanctification is a lifelong process wrought from God's Hand. As Christians, we must obey the Truth—we must! (Rom 6:15–16). True obedience can only happen through the Power of the Holy Spirit exposing one to the Truth of God's Word in its full integrity. Pray hard brothers and sisters, pray with tears streaming down your face (Eph 6:17--18), that you can have the precious and valuable fruit of self-control (Gal 5:22–23), for the start and finish of Sanctification is the process of growth, and the results of this growth is the power to separate oneself from sin and to consecrate oneself for the services of the Kingdom of God. We must be growing, not reclining and withering (Jn 15:6). We must be growing and developing supernaturally by actively pursuing obedience (Mt 6:33) as the Word manifests in our life for the common good through the Spirit of God who is good (1 Cor 12:7, Rom 8:28). Our Sanctification is dependent on the operation and energizing influence of the Holy Spirit to bring our redeemed lives into full conformity with Christ (Rom 8:29), who is the exact imprint of our Father and the radiance of His Glory (Heb 1:3). Finally, we will never obey the Truth of God apart from the power, grace, and assistance of the Holy Ghost enabling us, as individuals, to carry out the things that are naturally contrary to our sinful nature. By Grace and for our Sanctification and Glorification, we have been set apart for Redemption Through Christ Jesus (Jn 6:44, Jn 6:60–66).

Acts 17:28 New International Version (NIV)

[28] 'For in him we live and move and have our being.' As some of your own poets have said, 'We are his offspring

This extended essay is written to show that our Sanctification is God's Will (Thes 4:3). He set forth His Law for us all as His Elect (Lv 18:26)—we are chosen for Reconciliation and Redemption Through the Son's Blood (Rom 5:6–11) because we are Adopted (Eph 1:5) by God. Therefore, the reality of this should be a reason in itself for us to live blameless lives. We have the knowledge of God's Kingdom (Mt 13:11). We need to guard against all corruption of our souls. Truly, although we are in the land of corruption and biblical confusion in which the Truth is relative to most: "What is true for you is true for you, and what is true for me is true for me." Therefore, we are adopted by God and must be separate from all corruption, impurity, defilement, wickedness, and evil thereof. I tell you, let the mark of love distinguish you, all brothers and sisters, knowing that true love opposes sin, division, perversion, and deception, which are contradictory to love and tear down the fabric of love. Jesus says, ***(John 15:12-14)***[12] ***"This is my commandment, that you love one another as I have loved you.*** [13] ***Greater love has no one than this, that someone lay down his life for his friends.*** [14] ***You are my friends if you do what I command you.***

Beloved and only Begotten Son is rich in Love and Mercy. He Sanctified Himself so that He could sanctify us (Jn 17:19). He is the Truth incarnate and the Word made flesh (2 Jn 1:7). He was sanctified before there was creation (Eph 1:4), before there was light, and the earth was formless and void (Gen 1:1), but His Word of Truth was sanctified for us in His coming, when he, God, dwelt among us (Is 7:14). We all may partake in the benefits of His sanctified Word of Truth, which upholds the universe (Heb 1:3). The whole foundation of His Church is infinite and unified by the Power of His Word. The apostle and prophets have built on that foundation (Eph 2:20) and everything hinges on Christ, Who is the Cornerstone that the builders rejected (Mt 21:42). He, Christ, our Precious Lord, has become the Cornerstone in which our holy, sanctified, consecrated, and sacred Faith lives to this very day and until eternity.

The Revelation is that we all need to gain Authentic Righteousness (Mt 5:20, 6:33, 6:16–19, 6:14, 13:47–49, Jn 14:15, 2 Tm 3:1–8, 1 Pt 2:22, Heb 12:11). Jesus gave us His Word to lead us in everything Holy and Righteous so that we can be Sanctified by His Word and by the Truth of His Word. A transformation must take place in the heart, affecting our words, our thoughts, and our actions. Even our will and the desires and motives of our hearts must be transformed and quickened to know God, serve God, and surrender to God's Headship—one must have the regeneration happen instantaneously. The Spirit of God in the souls of men and women, the believers, must be quickened and transformed (2 Cor 3:18) by the Word in order to claim Sanctification through Saving Faith. For the vail has been taken away and we see the Glory of God, Jesus is Lord! And He is Sovereign over life, death, judgment, and all matter, even the fish we catch. He has Supreme Authority, and those who Love Him, Obey Him, and Fall Under His Lordship (Mt 12:30, Jn 14:15).

Our Justification. Our Justification is by God's Grace and through Faith in Christ alone (Rom 5:15–17), all enabled by the Sustaining Power of the Holy Spirit (1 Cor 6:11). Not by works, merits, tuition, or the law have we been imputed righteousness, but only by the Sinless Son of God (Rom 3:20). Amen. What are we saved from? We are saved from the condemnation of the law and the Just Judgment of God (Ez 7:1–27). We have been Justified before the judgment seat of Almighty God (Ps 9:1–10). God actually gave His Son out of Love to make propitiation for our sin, and the Son fulfilled the Father's demand in love by His Great Sacrifice of Atonement (Rom 3:25–26). This is why Christ says, "I and the Father are one" (Jn 10:30); they have the same Purpose and Will and Plan in perfect unity. The three persons of the Trinity unite in the same saving enterprise to seek and save the lost sheep of the flock (Ez 34:11–12). Jesus's perfect and continuous Life of Righteousness (1 Pet 2:22) merited Him Eternal Life, for His Labor was not in vain, and He transfers the fruits of His Labor to whoever believes and has faith; truly, we rest upon His refuge from the Condemnation of the Law and God's Wrath—it is the only way for salvation that is given to humanity (Acts 4:12). We believe. Hallelujah! Hosanna in the Highest! Justification allows us to have right standing with the Father by the forgiveness of our sin by the new covenant promise of Grace (Heb 8:8–12). Christ covers the darkness of

Adam's sin as well as the sin debt we have accrued over our life (Mt 19:32–35). We have refuge from the Wrath of God to come. As His Just Judgment fills the Heavenly Courts, we will be covered in the Mercy (Is 51:16, Rom 4:7–8) and Grace of His Beloved Son's Righteousness. Before the Holiness of God, by God's Grace through Faith in Christ alone, and by the Enabling Power of the Holy Spirit, you have been saved (Phil 3:9). The Lord alone can transfer to our bankrupt account His Wage that He earned He gave to us as a gift (Rom 6:23). Isn't it His to share with whomever He wants? He alone can cover any amount of darkness with His Light. He is the one who has the Sovereign Authority to forgive sins (Mt 9:6) and to justify any sinner who repents, believes, and has faith, truly. Believe and repent of your sin and be justified today, this very hour. Come into a Covenant (Heb 8:12) Relationship because God is just and the Justifier (Rom 3:26). Amen.

We were chosen. For it is our only hope, brothers and sisters, that we were predestined (Ez 1:5) by the Father to partake of His Plan of Redemption (Acts 4:28) in His Son from eternity past (Eph 1:11). He chose a large group of people and gave them to the Son as a Love Gift (Jn 18:9). However, Scripture says that God has graciously and lovingly Chosen His Elect out of the world. God did not have to choose any one of us, but He did (Eph 1:4–9). Remember that this world is lost and under judgment, this world is condemned, and this world is on the broad path heading for destruction, but God, by His Infinite Mercy and Abundant Grace, has Chosen His Elect out of it (1 Pet 1:2). Just look around and rub your eyes. Among the ones who are heading for destruction, who are perishing eternally, a vast number have been chosen to be objects of God's Redemption Plan (2 Pet 1:10). Have you been chosen? Have you been called? Has God revealed Himself to you? Because when He does, it will be unmistakable (Mt 12:27, Is 65:1–3, 2 Pet 1:10).

People say, "Well, that's not fair that God reveals Himself to some and not to everyone." But just think, no one wants what's fair and just. Ultimately, fair and just is that we remain in the world and that we go the way of the world (Rom 12:1–2). In addition, fair is that we would get only justice for our treason and remain under the law and be condemned to hell forever. That is what fair is; isn't that what we all justly deserve? Because one crime makes us guilty and because to fulfill the Law, we need to live under the Law perfectly and continually right! What would be unfair would be some getting what they did not deserve, but instead of getting what we justly do deserve, God has allowed us to receive His Mercy and Grace and Compassion (Heb 8:12). We are Blessed that we have received His Divine Favor if we walk upright (Ps 84:11–12) through Faith in His Son's work. Because, when you look around, those who deny the Son of God will receive justice: The Son will deny them to the Father in the Heavenly Courts. Our God will not use injustice or un-righteousness for He is Pure and does no wrong (Dt 32:4); even His Wrath is just, even His Anger is Just, and even His Jealousy is Just and Righteous (Dt 32:3-4), but all will receive a Righteous and Just Judgment. Do you understand? All will receive a Just Judgment if they do not repent of their sin and believe in Jesus the Christ. If they reject Him before the Father (Jn 12:48), they are defiant and rebellious sinners, and God will then Judge them all Justly for their sins. But God has chosen some to adopt and call His Children, and He will use non-justice on them. He uses mercy, grace, and forgiveness; neither His love nor His justice is compromised one bit because He is Just and He is the Justifier.

God is Just, Compassionate, and Merciful to whomever He wishes, isn't it His Right to do so? (Rom 9:14–16). All who reject this Truth only believe that God is a little Sovereign, but the Scriptures unambiguously say He is Fully Sovereign and has Supreme Authority. It is His Right to choose us, isn't it? (1Tm 6:15–17). Of course, friend, God is Lord! When a parent goes to an orphanage, does the child choose the parent or the parent choose the child? Of course, the parent chooses the child; it is reasonable He Parents to adopt the child (Jn 15:16).

Exodus 33:19

And the LORD said, "I will cause all my goodness to pass in front of you, and I will proclaim my name, the ***LORD, in your presence. I will have mercy*** on ***whom I will*** **have mercy, and I will have compassion on whom I will have compassion.**

God chose you and appointed you (Jn 13:17–18) for holiness because He is Holy (Lv 11:44). He commands us to love because He is Love (1 Jn 4:1–6). And once He draws (Jn 6:44) us in by changing our heart and doing Supernatural Surgery on us (Ez 36:26–28), He saves us from the Condemnation of the Law by Grace Through His Son's Blood on our behalf. In Greek, the word *draws* in John 6:44 means drag, not entices or wowed, but drag. God must overcome our resistance to the Gospel. He drags us to the Truth, not kicking and screaming, but He does a work in our hearts and changes our desires by putting His Spirit in us and changing us from the inside (1 Jn 5:13–16). For we once resisted the Gospel_(1 Cor 15:3–10, Lk 24:46–49), but now we love and see the Compassion of God in His Son. He has given us new hearts and we are being powerfully drawn into a Saving Relationship (Rom 5:9–11). Not only do we have God's Grace, but we also have His Saving Grace (Eph 2:8). He gives us to His Son so that we have Faith in Him to Justify us, Sanctify us, Redeem us, and Reconcile us back to the Father and then Resurrect us in our glorified body for the Glory of God in His Son, Jesus (Rom 8:30). His Workmanship is our salvation (Eph 2:10); thus, we will be made just like Him in perfect Holiness and love. Truly, brothers and sisters, the elect have hope, our joy is in the Coming of Christ. Amen.

Covered by justification; cleaned by sanctification. If you are a believer, it is God's Sovereign Plan to form you and mold you into His Glorified Transformation (Jer 18:1–6). Our sanctification is the created work of the Godhead (Eph 4:24), and the willing labor of the believer actively perusing Authentic Righteousness comes from God Himself (Phil 2:13), for His Joy is in the obedience, love, and faithfulness of His Devoted Children

(1 Cor 7:5). For it was He who started the work in us and has promised to see the work completed in us, His Adopted Children (Phil 1:6), as an inward and outward work of the heart and the nature (Pt 1:4) of His Elect, leading the will of His Chosen People to the Obedience of the Spirit. We are all called to worship in Spirit and in Truth (Jn 4:24) and war against the flesh (1 Pt 2:11) to the Honor and Glory of God (Ps 29:2).

Justification is the covering of our sins before the Face of the Father so that we can be holy and presentable to come into His very presence (Rom 4:7–8). Justification is an alien righteousness, one that is not our own but shared with us freely as a gift (Phil 3:9), and our Scarification is where we grow in Authentic Righteousness, a Righteousness that is enabled by the Holy Spirit (1 Jn 3:10). Justification covers sin (Rom 4:7), whereas Sanctification washes away (Jer 4:14), cleanses (Heb 10:22) (1 Jn 1:7), and clears sin (Jn 1:29).

We must have a covering and a cleansing of sin. First, we need to be justified and enabled to come into the Presence of God and to be acceptable to Him. Righteousness was accredited to us, covering our unrighteousness before the Face of Holy God (Jn 12:13). By God's Grace, through Faith in Christ alone, He accredits righteousness to us and the Scripture was fulfilled: ***"Abraham believed God, and it was counted to him as righteousness"—and he was called a friend of God***.

Next we need the clearing of sin in our Sanctification to be made presentable; to be called Sons and Daughters of the Highest, we are commanded to practice righteousness (1 Jn 3:9) and to be holy and separate from all corruption (1 Jn 5:4). We are to live for His Glory and Honor and have the distinguishing mark of His Children —"holiness" (Lv 11:44) and "love" (1 Jn 4:7)—once we are accredited and/or imputed righteous by a transfer of Christ's Earned Merit of righteousness as a gift! Finally, we are being wrought, refined, and transformed to sustain Authentic Righteousness in and of our self. For we, as Christians, are the Workmanship of God. By the Lord's Holy Word and Divine

Truth, through prayer and worship, the Holy Ghost, the very Incarnation of God, is working in and through us. In this Christ sustains us by the Power of the Holy Spirit (Heb 1:3) because when we are with the Lord, He is with us and we abide in Him and He abides in us, but better yet, Jesus says, behold "I am with you always, to the end of the age" (Mt 28:20).

We are being wrought by God's Sovereign, Providential Hand-crafted workmanship, and when the Lord's Second Coming is here, the trumpet will sound and we will rejoin with our spiritual body and be Resurrected and Glorified (1 Cor 14:52–56) as people who gave all their Glory to God. We will actually be righteous like Christ; His work of reconciliation did not come back void but fulfilled and successful. Our predestined life as men and women on this planet is to bring Glory to God through our words, our thoughts, and our actions and, yes, even the motive of our hearts; we bring Honor and Glory to Our Father because it is due His Name, forever. Sanctification is living life before the Face of God and living a life that is pleasing to God. By speaking and acting in love, thinking about love, and desiring to love and be loved and spreading the fame of Jesus, Our Savior, to the world by revealing His Love, this is Righteousness, friends.

We read in Scripture that Christ is washing away our sins (1 Cor 6:11) and cleansing us (Ez 36:25) from all unrighteousness in the Sanctification of our souls, our beliefs, our attitudes, our thoughts, our desires, our actions, and our words. He is Sanctifying our hearts, minds, bodies, doctrine, emotions, natures, and, yes, even our will. Our purposes, values, ethics, morals, plans, and, yes, even the culture we live in are all being sanctified by the Lord. We are all a work in progress and will come into alignment and conformity to God (Jn 8:51) in the biblical culture that is the Lord's will for you: "your holiness." This is your separation from sin by forgiveness, for love covers a multitude of sin. The Truth exposes our wrongs? Yes, the Law cuts us to the knees, but Christ enables us to turn from our sins and clears them away from our life so we can walk upright. Although we fall seven times seventy-seven times, we rise. However, God wants us to walk upright, not fall.

We will be Holy and Righteous on the day of our Lord's Coming and will be blameless before the Lord, by His Blood, which covers us and washes us as white as snow, truly. We will shine as bright as the sun (Acts 26:13–14) in our Glorified bodies on the day the trumpet sounds and our Spirit that the Father made alive for Eternity in His Joy (1 Jn 5:11–12) is rejoined to our spiritual bodies and resurrected (1 Cor 15:44–45).

Covered / clothed in righteousness.

Romans 4:6-8 New International Version (NIV)

[6] David says the same thing when he speaks of the blessedness of the one to whom God credits righteousness apart from works:

[7] "Blessed are those
whose transgressions are forgiven,
whose sins are covered.
[8] Blessed is the one
whose sin the Lord will never count against them."

Galatians 3:26-28 New International Version (NIV)

[26] So in Christ Jesus you are all children of God through faith, [27] for all of you who were baptized into Christ have clothed yourselves with Christ. [28] There is neither Jew nor Gentile, neither slave nor free, nor is there male and female, for you are all one in Christ Jesus.

Obey and Have Victory. Although we will never be perfect in this life (Rom 7:15, Phil 3:12), we will always rely on the Grace of God to carry us to the Gates of Heaven. Meanwhile, the war is all around us, and we need to be aware of our enemy and take up the Armor of God (Eph 6:10–20) and fight the battle that lies before us, every day, all as Abiding Disciples of Jesus Christ (Jn 15:5), our King. Have victory each of you, prevail over the satanic assault and influences, and prevail over Satan himself; be victorious (1 Jn 5:4–5) because the Elect has the Armor of God (Eph 6:10–20). Sorry to sound crass, but check yourselves, if you do not hate sin, you are not a Christian. Is that too harsh to say? (Jn 8:34–35, Am 5:15). If you do not hate lies, deceit, gossip, and slander against your neighbor or family member, you are not a Christian. Jesus hates evil (Heb 1:9). Is this too harsh to say? Because these are the very weapons of the dark angels and the evil one's stronghold on our lives (2 Cor 10:4–6). Fight and call on the Name of the Lord, always; He is with you, when you are with Him, especially in times of strategic warfare and battle (Ps 18:3).

A brief introduction to Sanctification is our lesson today, talking about the difference between Justification and Sanctification, as well as our need for a covering and washing of sin, is for your benefit, Christian. Wisdom and discernment are necessary; ask and He will give you all the wisdom you will need (Mt 6:15–23). Scripture says, ***the beginning of wisdom is the fear of the Lord*** (Prv 9:10). He is the King, and the King wants victory, not cowardly submission to the enemy or treason, with one foot in and one foot out (Rom 6:15–23), but our mighty King wants victory. After all, isn't it His Will, Purpose, and Plan for His People to succeed in everything Holy, Righteous, and Godly, all to the Father's Glory (Prv 3:1–12). Amen.

John 14:23-24 New International Version (NIV)

[23]Jesus replied, "***Anyone who loves me will obey my teaching. My Father will love them, and we will come to them and make our home with them.*** [24]***Anyone who does not love me will not obey my teaching. These words you hear are not my own; they belong to the Father who sent me.***

John 14:21 New International Version (NIV)

[21] ***Whoever has my commands and keeps them is the one who loves me. The one who loves me will be loved by my Father, and I too will love them and show myself to them.***"

John 15:14 New International Version (NIV)

[14] ***You are my friends if you do what I command.***

Our dear Lord's prayer to His Father on the night of His Betrayal, the very night before His crucifixion.

Priestly Prayer:

NIV John 17:15-19

> ***My prayer is not that you take them out of the world but that you protect them from the evil one. 16 They are not of the world, even as I am not of it. 17 Sanctify them by the truth; your word is truth. 18 As you sent me into the world, I have sent them into the world. 19 For them I sanctify myself, that they too may be truly sanctified.***

I want to thank Christine Gauthier for the
kind support in Editing this book.
Blessings for the next books to come.
To the Glory of God!

Printed in the United States
By Bookmasters